A
PSYCHOLOGIST'S
CHILDHOOD

BY THE SAME AUTHOR

From Tests to Therapy

A PSYCHOLOGIST'S CHILDHOOD

AT THE DAWN OF COGNITIVE BEHAVIOUR THERAPY

G. ALAN SMITH

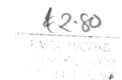

Matador
9 Priory Business Park
Wistow Road
Kibworth
Leicester LE8 0RX, UK
Tel: (+44) 116 279 2299
Fax: (+44) 116 279 2277
Email: books@troubador.co.uk
Web: www.troubador.co.uk/matador

ISBN 978 1783060 900

British Library Cataloguing in Publication Data.
A catalogue record for this book is available from the British Library.

Printed and bound in the UK by TJ International, Padstow, Cornwall
Typeset in 11pt Palatino by Troubador Publishing Ltd, Leicester, UK

Matador is an imprint of Troubador Publishing Ltd

To those who helped me

CONTENTS

INTRODUCTION

Survey reveals mental health ignorance among teenagers. This was a recent headline that seemed both surprising and yet also unsurprising. Anyone who has had experience of (or contact with) mental illness discovers how little they know about such things. And indeed how little is known by most people, at any age. However, it is true that adolescence is a particularly vulnerable time of life, when we need better defences against psychological problems. Is there any way that this question could be given more attention in schools, perhaps?

In my own adolescence (fifty years ago), I was a successful student at a good school, but knew absolutely nothing about mental health until it was too late. Despite having an upbringing that was not particularly unusual, with no really terrible experiences, I developed a significant problem (social anxiety disorder and depression) which led to a compulsory stay in a mental hospital for several months. My eyes were opened, not only to my own ignorance and the ignorance of my family and school, but also to the questionable nature of the professional services available. In fact it could be argued that my entire problem was generated and maintained by ignorance.

Fifty years later, after undoubted progress in psychiatry and psychology, good work by mental health charities, and all sorts of information campaigns on television and radio, you would expect us all to be much wiser now. But of course we are not. When it comes to mental health, we are all teenagers. We don't want to know what's good for us. We don't want to admit to having any problems. We don't want to look bad in the eyes of others. And we don't like to admit that we don't understand these things.

Despite all this ignorance, most people do manage to solve their own problems, although perhaps suffering an unnecessary amount of difficulty and hardship in the process. In my case, while working out my own solutions I glimpsed an interesting possibility of solving similar problems for other people. At an age when I was looking for a career in some sort of science, it became almost inevitable that I would end up as a clinical psychologist.

Some unkind people, as well as pointing a critical finger at mental illness, also scoff at mental health workers. *Just trying to solve their own problems*, they say. Well, in my case I can reject that. By that time, I had already solved my problems, and this had inspired me to want to solve some more. The other cynical accusation sometimes made against mental health workers is that they just have a *need to help people* (as if that is a bad thing). Indeed one of my tutors at university, when I was applying to do a clinical psychology course, advised me not to say that I wanted to help people, otherwise they would think I was some kind of *do-gooder*. Having originally wished to become a mathematician, I was quite happy to go along with the idea that solving problems could be a purely intellectual exercise. However, I did hope secretly that some people would be helped by my efforts.

The book tells the story of my childhood and adolescence in Tyneside, in the North-East of England, with particular focus on the development of my social anxiety disorder and depression. A real case history can be more illuminating than vague generalities. Alongside the autobiography I have added a psychological commentary, which of course has the benefit of hindsight as well as many years of experience as a clinical psychologist. But at the time I was just *following my nose*. You don't have to be a psychologist to do that.

The intention of the book, as well as simply telling my story, is to illustrate how modern cognitive behavioural therapy is rooted in elementary common sense and natural behaviour. Even a teenager might be able to work these things out for himself. Don't be overawed by the psychological jargon. For example *Cognitive Behavioural* simply means thoughts and actions working in combination, and is really just a loosely applied brand name for these types of therapy. My story shows that I (and no doubt many others) were able to apply cognitive behavioural principles long before anyone had ever heard of CBT.

FIRST MEMORIES

1948

According to my mother, this event happened when I was about three years old. Now that I am in my sixties, I do not directly remember it at all, except for having vaguely remembered it for a moment at the age of seventeen. That was when I checked it out with my mother, because it felt more like a dream than a memory. The events occurred at Whitley Bay, on the Northumberland coast just above the mouth of the Tyne. We were on a family outing, probably on a Sunday afternoon, sitting on the sands with a view of the grey and white waves coming in from the North Sea. However, my only memory was of being inside a large wooden hut, where I was standing on some kind of platform, with people staring at me. And then a little later I remember being on the way home, with my mother scolding my father for falling asleep and not taking proper care of me. She had a very sharp edge to her voice.

It seems that my mother had got bored with sitting on the beach, and had taken my older sister up to the promenade and shops, leaving my father in charge while I played with the sand. Unfortunately he became too relaxed and fell asleep, so naturally I toddled off along the beach unrestrained. That was how I ended up as the centre of attention in the Lost Children's Shelter. When my mother returned and found my father blissfully asleep, no doubt she panicked and eventually ran to the Shelter. On the way home I remember my father apologising, but defending himself with the fact that he had been hard at work all week, in order to make enough money to support us all, and that was why he had fallen asleep.

Fortunately no harm was done, apart from giving everyone a fright. I have no memory of what I felt, apart from that puzzlement about where I was and what was going on.

1949

At about four years old, I was the proud owner of a blue tricycle. We lived on the corner of Nansen Street in Consett (County Durham), and unfortunately there was nowhere for me to ride it safely unaccompanied. So while my mother was busy with her housework, I rode round and round the front room. This room had been left unfurnished and with bare floorboards, perhaps to provide me with a playroom or perhaps because the family finances had not stretched that far. The boards had been painted or varnished in a two-foot wide strip around the edge of the room, so that a large rug or piece of carpet normally would have been placed over the untreated floorboards in the middle (this was many years before the arrival of fitted carpets for the masses).

I placed my front wheel to follow the inner edge of the varnished strip, and rode round the room until boredom and fatigue set in. But instead of then giving up, I raised the stakes by going faster, until I was circling the whole room in only a few seconds. This must have caused the floorboards to vibrate noisily, and my mother appeared. *Are you not tired of just going round and round like that?* By this time I was indeed totally fatigued, but I was not going to admit it to anyone, and carried on doing a few more circuits just to show off. But mother knows best, and after a little while I did give up.

Although I was too young to be allowed to play outside the

house at Nansen Street, there was an area of roadway at the side where older local boys sometimes came to kick a football. One afternoon, they were kicking it against the side wall of our house, causing a thumping noise inside, which went on and on repeatedly for a long time, until my mother grew extremely tense and shouted *I can't stand this any longer, I'll have to go and tell them.* But it seemed to me that she was nervous about challenging these boys, so I too felt fearful. However, she did go outside and told them to move off, and perhaps they were cheeky to her. When my father came home from work, she persuaded him to go and see the parents of these boys to make sure they did not come back. His mission was successful, and there were no more footballs, at least not against the wall of our house.

Childhood amnesia *refers to the fact that people remember virtually nothing from before the age of three or so, and any memories from the following few years tend to be very sketchy (Weir, K. 2011). This is despite the fact that during these early years we are picking up many complex skills such as the ability to walk, talk and recognise people's faces. And children as young as two or three do recall events at the time, but then these memories fade away.*

One part of the explanation is that the structures in the brain which deal with memory are still developing and changing during these years. Another factor is that autobiographical memory depends upon having the words to describe an experience (at the time of having that experience), and of course our vocabulary is very poorly developed at an early age. However, if parents talk about events in a richly detailed and repeated manner, this helps the child to remember them.

It is not clear whether a person's earliest memories really have any special significance, but still it is tempting to regard the experiences that have survived through the mists of time as being important in some way. My own early memories seem to involve various discomforts: people staring at me, my mother's sharp tongue, keeping myself going in the face of fatigue, and my mother's fear. It is possible to see these themes continuing during the following years.

2

MOTHER TAKES CHARGE

1949

One morning when I came downstairs for breakfast, I found my parents and sister sitting at the kitchen table looking ill at ease. The curtains were drawn, even though it was daylight and the sun was shining through them. I hesitated only a second before asking the obvious question: *Why are the curtains drawn?* My mother's voice was strangely hushed: *Your grandma's passed away.* This was not a phrase that I understood. Four-year-olds ask a lot of questions, so I did not hesitate: *What's happened?* My sister put on her best grown-up expression (she was ten) and explained: *She's died.* I was none the wiser really, but sensed that this line of questioning was not getting anywhere. In any case, death did not seem very interesting, especially if it was something that happened to these old people. I was more interested in why the curtains were drawn, and repeated my question about this. *It's so that people will know that we've got a funeral today, and they won't come and bother us,* my mother explained.

This grandma was my father's mother, my other grandparents having died during the war years, before I was born. So my grandad was now living alone, and it soon emerged that he wished (indeed demanded) someone to move in with him, to do the housekeeping. That housekeeper would be a woman, of course, either his daughter or his daughter-in-law (my mother). It seems that this was a common arrangement in those days, an expectation even, and my dad felt a particular obligation. As the eldest son, and especially as he was employed by his father, he felt that it would be reasonable to move us into grandad's house, where the family plumbing business was based. My mother could then do the cleaning and cooking for everyone. However, my mother had considerable doubts about this, especially as she felt that my father was already too much under grandad's thumb. In fact she didn't much care for grandad, and when she mentioned him at all she called him *the ould devil*. In particular, she regarded him as greedy, exploiting my father by making him work long hours for very little pay.

But my father persuaded her to give it a try, just for two weeks to see what it was like. We went to stay at grandad's house just a few streets away in Sherburn Terrace, Consett. My mother set to work cleaning the old range, a stove with a coal fire and two ovens. Meanwhile I amused myself on my own, which seemed to irritate grandad, leading him to snap at my mother: *The boy shouldn't be in here, he should be outside playing football or something, otherwise he'll grow up soft!* That may have been the final straw. My mother was not going to put up with the ould devil dictating how her children should be brought up. I could detect her mood lightening, as she realised that this gave her the perfect excuse to say that she was not going to live with grandad.

Secretly, of course, my father felt just the same and had no real wish to live with grandad, but he had not liked to say so. He was now happy to let my mother take this decision, and she was pleased to feel that she had won that battle. She wanted a house of her own, with a husband who was less ruled by his father, and the freedom to bring up her children to be something better than any of them. She had said No to a potential prison, and had got her way.

Fortunately, the situation was eased rapidly when it emerged that my aunt and her husband were actually quite happy to go to live with grandad. They had a house on the outskirts of Consett, not far from Shotley Bridge, and my parents were able to buy it from them. These were the days when you could get a mortgage and buy a house even with quite a low income, although I think they had borrowed a deposit from my grandad. So now we moved to this nice modern house with bay windows in Cutlers Hall Road. My mother was glad to get away from the back streets of Consett, a rather grim town which had been created around the Iron Works and suffered from its pollution. *You hang your washing out on a Monday, and it can end up covered in red dust,* she explained. But now I had a garden and some space to play outside, and very soon I would be starting school. The school near to our new house would be better than the one in the middle of Consett, my mother said, pleased with her achievement of this aim. Clearly there is nothing new about the idea of getting a better school for your child by moving to a better neighbourhood.

But just after the move I suffered a bitter blow. One evening my mother announced: *There's a man coming just now to buy the tricycle.* Hang on, I thought, that's *my* tricycle, it's my old friend, indeed my only friend. *There's nowhere here to ride it, being on a steep hill, and you haven't actually used it for a while now,* she pointed out. *Anyway, you're getting a bit big for it now that you're nearly ready to go to school.* I felt as if I was being robbed, but managed to control myself while the man arrived and inspected the tricycle, trying to haggle over the price. But my mother insisted on the full £5 (a week's wages for my father in those days), and the man handed over the banknotes.

When he had gone I complained: *why did you not tell me you were going to sell it? It was mine.* She explained that she had wanted to avoid upsetting me. *We're a bit short of money at the moment, with the new house needing a lot doing to it.* That was my first lesson in the harsh realities of money. All of our money came from my father's wages, which in turn were painfully extracted from grandad and the plumbing business. My mother was like most married women in those days, and never went out to work. As a child I would be a drain on the family finances until I grew up and got a job. So my mother would have to say No to my childish expectations, just like she had said No to grandad.

This was the first time that I became conscious of being a financial liability, a debt that threatened to hang over me until I was old enough to go out to work and bring money home. Over the years, my mother frequently mentioned the fact that she had no choice but to run a very tight household budget, because of my father's low wages. Her own father had been a coal miner, with a relatively good income and only one child, so when she married into the family plumbing business she had been surprised to find herself worse off. She made sure that my father handed over the weekly pay packet to her, and then she gave him just enough pocket money to buy his tobacco ration. After that it was up to her to pay all the bills and do the shopping.

Assertiveness *is the psychological jargon term for saying No to people (Bishop, S. 2006). Or more precisely it is when you simply declare your own rights or point of view, neither aggressively threatening the rights of others nor submissively allowing others to ignore or deny your interests.*

In 1949, most women were financially and socially dependent upon their husbands, and it could take a lot of courage for them to have minds of their own. Of course, not all husbands wished to have submissive wives, but even so it was important for women to develop the art of expressing their views, without fear but also without causing trouble.

Being assertive is not the same as being antagonistic or aggressive. The latter is often considered to be part of the dark side of human nature, and indeed it can lead to events such as murder and war and all the terrible things that people do to each other. Nevertheless, it is essential to become skilled in the more reasonable forms of antagonism, in order to stay safe while coping with the perils of life. A friendly or caring attitude is hopefully your main preference in life, but there can be occasions when this would place you in danger from people who have no such care. That is when you might have to go on the offensive (or at least the defensive) to protect yourself.

In order to protect yourself from manipulation by other people, you need to be firm and say tough things (like No). It is remarkable how many people cannot do this, becoming easy meat for predators such as doorstep salesmen or telesales callers. Unassertive (too polite) people feel very anxious or guilty about saying no. They give in to the other person, and say whatever is necessary in order to appease them. However, this is only a short term solution which eventually they regret, with the realisation that their good nature has been abused. But then they silently bottle up this anger for a long time, until it comes out in some kind of irrational explosion.

Assertiveness is a much more effective strategy. First, you identify the fact that this other person is affecting you adversely or trying to take advantage of your good nature. Then you decide that you need to fend them off, to prevent any further harm or offence. Remember that you are perfectly entitled to do so. They may be entitled to ask something of you, but you are equally entitled to refuse. So just say no, as simply and clearly as possible, in a manner that is expressive but calm and controlled. Tough but cool. Polite, but not too polite (if they see any sign of weakness, they may persist in trying to get round you, and you will have to say no all over again).

My mother had now gathered confidence in her ability to take charge of her own family, and to sort people out while keeping them reasonably happy. Unfortunately, there is sometimes a danger of taking assertiveness a step too far. Success in exerting power against others can be corrupted into coercive nagging, emotional blackmail, and bullying. That would be rather nasty, wouldn't it?

3

WHAT A GOOD BOY

1950

I had reached the age for starting school. In those days there were very few pre-school or nursery facilities, so a child's big step into the outside world did not take place until the age of five. It was a significant step for my mother as well, of course, freeing her (or at least leaving her at home on her own) after eleven years of looking after my sister and then me.

Fortunately the school was not far away, on Benfieldside Road, just a short climb up Backstone Burn, the steep lane behind our house, and then across the main road and through the gates. There was very little traffic in those days, so it was a very safe walk which I would do on my own quite happily a little later on. But on the first day, of course, my mother clutched my hand to lead me across the road.

1951

My main memories of the Infants School (age 5 to 7) are to do with reading and writing. Most children manage to learn to read and write at this stage, and indeed a few might start school already equipped with quite a good reading ability. Usually this is because their mothers have spent time showing them the basics, as well as simply reading to them. Some teachers frown on this amateur tuition, arguing that the child may be taught the wrong habits or learn by a different method to that which is used at the school. However, others argue that it is very valuable to have interest and input of any kind from the parent.

In my case, my mother had taught me a very useful amount of reading and writing before starting school, and probably I spent quite a bit of time on my own with books. No doubt she wished to give me a head start in life, so that I could take full advantage of the improved educational opportunities which were part of the new era following the Second World War. She herself had left school at the age of 14, having achieved a fair amount of literacy and arithmetical skills, in contrast to her mother who was illiterate and signed her name with a cross. My father had left school even earlier, at the age of 12, to become an apprentice plumber, and his reading and writing was adequate but lacking in confidence. My mother's ambitions for me may have been influenced by her own father, who had been a Durham coal miner. Many miners had a strong tradition of self-improvement through the Workers' Educational Association, and were surprisingly talented.

I am sure that my apparent cleverness was greatly pleasing to my mother, but at school I learned that pleasing people was not always so simple. One day the teacher wrote a little story on the blackboard, telling us to copy this out in our exercise books. She was expecting us to take a good length of time, giving her some peace to do some work of her own. Instead, I thought this task was terribly easy, and wrote it all out in just a few minutes. Thinking that this would impress the teacher, I rushed up to her desk with my work. Surprised, she told me off. I had done it too quickly and not in my best possible handwriting. *Look, everyone else is doing it more carefully. Do it again.* Deflated, I went back to my desk, and took revenge by writing in an exaggerated and ridiculously slow manner, taking care not to finish before the rest of the class. *Much better*, she said, this time with a glint of humour. She knew that she had taught me something more than reading and writing.

1952

You also learn from other children. I was sitting behind another boy one day, and he decided to demonstrate his skills in behavioural observation. He turned round to look at me, and I smiled at him, as you do. After a few minutes he turned round again, and I smiled again. He and I repeated this several times, and finally he gave me a name: *We're going to call you Smiler!* Wondering if I was being insulted, I asked him why. *Every time I look at you, you smile. Other people don't keep smiling like that.* I wonder if he ever became a behavioural psychologist. After that, I became a little self-conscious about my smiling habit. But I liked having a smile, and it soon resumed.

Each week we listened to one of the Schools Programmes on the radio (or the wireless, as it was called then). Out of the blue one morning, the announcer cut in with the news that the King (George VI) had died. When I walked home at lunchtime, I was bursting with this news. *Did you know the King's dead?* My mother was sceptical about this, and how could I possibly know such a thing. *You might have got it wrong. Anyway, we'll listen to the news on the wireless tonight, and see if anything has happened.* It never occurred to my mother that she could listen to the wireless during the day. That was reserved for after 6 o'clock in the evening. I was proved to be correct, of course. The King was dead, and I was a good boy.

1953

One day my mother was startled by my sudden question: *Are you and da my real parents?* Another child at school, or maybe the teacher, had revealed the possibility that you can be adopted. For some reason, this explained a lot to me. You are supposed to resemble at least one of your parents, whereas I had been getting a feeling that I might be a bit different to these people that I lived with. Already my success at school was giving me ideas above my station. But my mother was indignant: *Of course we are your real parents! Whatever made you ask that?* So I had to forget that theory. You have to believe your mother, don't you?

1953

That wasn't the only fact of life that I was introduced to, by some lad walking my way home from school, on the steps down to Backstone Burn. One particular boy seemed to have a hotline to the adult world. *You know we all die, don't you?* That was his whispered message one day. This was news to me, and I was about to deny it, but then I remembered grandma and realised that it might be true. For a moment life looked too bleak to be worth the effort, but I didn't know what to do with that thought, and it passed.

A few weeks later my friend had more news for me. *You know the difference between boys and girls, don't you?* Of course I do, I was about to say, thinking of how girls had long hair and silly voices. But he was insistent on telling me the gruesome facts. *You know how boys have willies to pee with? Well, girls just have a little slit.* Don't be ridiculous, he's surely wrong, I thought. Someone has told him this for a laugh. *If you don't believe me, wait till you're older and you'll see that I'm right,* he assured me with all the authority of a nine-year-old.

The nature-nurture question is the age-old issue of whether human beings are born with in-built characteristics such as their abilities or personality, or whether we start out as a blank slate which absorbs our experiences and learning. The usual answer has always been that both influences are important to some degree, but there have been various fashions in the amount of emphasis given to one or the other. During the post-war years there was an increasing enthusiasm for attempting to modify ourselves, either by self-improvement or by social measures such as universal education and health care. More recently (Pinker,

S. 2002) *we have been reminded that human behaviour is substantially shaped by evolutionary psychological adaptations, which are there in all of us. We will have a greater success in modifying ourselves if we take into account the given limits and potentials of our human nature.*

At the age of eight I did not understand any of this, of course. As a good little scholar, I was absorbing not only literacy and mathematical skills, but also a general view of the world much wider than my parents could have had. This had already triggered an uneasy sense of alienation from them, as I had no knowledge of their family histories and the inadequate schooling which had led to these differences between us. And I was not yet sophisticated enough to be able to see the deeper similarities in our nature.

This might also be seen in terms of a generation gap, which was actually larger than average in my case, as my parents had delayed my conception for six years until the end of the War (having had my sister in 1939). There had been two world wars during their lifetime before I appeared, and a great deal had changed in society (but not in human nature). It was not surprising that I felt different to my parents.

Listening to others *is an important skill in life, being a key way of learning from other people. It is a short cut to knowledge and wisdom, as otherwise you would have to discover everything for yourself. There are other ways of acquiring information, of course (for example reading, which is the equivalent in a visual mode). Like everything else we do, listening can also be done badly, leading you into all sorts of errors.*

There are various attitudes that you can adopt to try to make better sense of people's words. A skilled listener chooses how to listen, and selects an approach appropriate to the occasion. The most basic approach is to absorb simply whatever is said, without question. You swallow it whole and it becomes part of you. Children are the most likely to do this, although we can all do it at times. There is a danger that you will end up believing false or inaccurate information. However, it is not always a bad thing. For example, if you are trying to learn a new skill, and you trust the instructor, it might proceed more quickly if you just do what you are told.

The opposite of this is cynicism, which is when you are set to disbelieve everything you hear. You might even question things that are perfectly reasonable. Perhaps this attitude develops sometimes from the shock that everyone experiences sooner or later, when you discover that a friend, parent, or other trusted person has led you up the garden path. You resolve never to be deceived again, although hopefully you will relax about this after time has passed without too much further trouble.

A humorous attitude can help you to compromise between excessive belief and excessive disbelief. Unfortunately a state of stress can cause you to lose your sense of humour, just when you need it most. In this mode of listening, you are actively looking for any humorous angle that you can put upon the other person's words. This helps to detach yourself from what you have heard, while perhaps considering whether to take it seriously.

Re-listening from memory is a useful back-up. Pay attention to what the person actually says (rather than what you assume he means), so that you can replay his words later, perhaps finding another meaning.

At the age of seven or eight, a child needs to listen and learn, in a fairly sponge-like manner. Hopefully adults will be kind and honest, and not fill children's ears with too much nonsense. I was a good little boy and enjoyed listening to adults such as teachers, who rewarded me with praise so that I would listen even more. By listening to them, I was discovering a world completely different to that of my parents. By listening to other children, I was discovering that adults don't tell you everything.

4

DOWN BY THE RIVER

1953

It was quite a short walk downhill from our house to Shotley Bridge, a pleasant little village on the outskirts of Consett. At school we had been told about the ancient history of sword-making at the old Cutlers Hall at Shotley Bridge, but as a young lad I was more interested in the river Derwent which flowed under the said Bridge. It was quite a shallow river, with lots of rock pools with crystal clear water and grassy banks, a paradise for a small boy.

I soon took to fishing which, at the age of eight, meant scooping up minnows into a jam jar. The technique was to tie a string tightly around the neck of the jar, place the jar under the water lying on its side, and then wait for a minnow to swim into it. This took a certain amount of patience, but small boys seem to be quite happy staring into pools of water, and I was no exception. The string was then pulled to lift the jar out quickly before the minnow escaped. Each minnow was transferred to another jar, until there were about half a dozen, which were then carried home with pride to be kept in a goldfish bowl.

Eventually however, I discovered that these minnows did not seem to survive very long in captivity, at least not in a crude goldfish bowl, and rather reluctantly I gave up this pursuit. Instead, I realised that I was content simply watching these little fish darting about amongst the rocks and stones. And that was what I was doing one afternoon, sitting crouched on a rock in the middle of the stream, when I realised with horror that I was slipping slowly backwards into the water. Suddenly my bottom felt very cold and wet, and then I was standing up to my knees in the river. After clambering up the bank watched by my parents and sister, it was obvious that we would have to go home. They had a good laugh at my dripping pants, as I walked along feeling a public embarrassment that I had never felt before.

One part of the river at Shotley Bridge was quite different. It was known as *The Rocks*, for obvious reasons, being an area of rock terraces with the river tumbling fast through a narrow gap in the middle. Many children and their families would gather there to sit or play on sunny weekends, and sometimes it was so crowded that my mother would say it was *like Blackpool beach*. The river was about four feet wide through the gap in the rocks, and boys challenged each other to jump across it. As I stood watching the frighteningly fast flow of the water deep below, an older boy asked if I was going to try it. *No, I think I would be frightened of falling in,* I said, very honestly. My mother was always frightened that I would fall in somewhere. But the older boy was gently encouraging: *Do you think you can jump that far on dry land? If you ignore the water, it's just the same distance.* So I jumped, and it was no problem. Jumping back was even easier. It is surprising what you can learn from other children.

It was possible to walk all along the riverbank for several miles, as far as Ebchester. I became quite keen to go walking in this countryside, but now there was the aim of collecting wild flowers. This idea had been started off by one of the teachers at school, who had organised a competition to put together the biggest and best pressed wild flower collection. The idea was to identify and learn the names of these plants, using books borrowed from the public library. This seemed to me like a really interesting game, and I did not realise that it was my first introduction to homework.

It was also my first introduction to competitiveness. In those days it was easier than it is now to find a huge variety of plants on the river bank or in hedgerows or fields. After several weeks of walks, my album was stuffed full of flowers, all flattened and neatly labelled. The teacher looked very impressed, and I was declared the winner. The following year, I did the same and won again. This did not lead to any great interest in botany, but my competitiveness did remain.

From Shotley Bridge, the river Derwent runs north-east all the way to the Tyne, and the main road roughly follows it. My mother liked to travel on the bus to Newcastle to visit the shops there, and sometimes she would take me with her. The road passed through Ebchester, Hamsterley, Lintzford, Rowlands Gill, and Winlaton Mill, and at one place there was a turning with a sign to Chopwell. My mother always pointed at this and said in a hushed voice: *There used to be a lot of communists living down there. My father knew all about them.* Apparently Chopwell was known as *little Moscow* in the 1930s due to the socialist policies of the local miners' union, and clearly my grandfather (as a staunch Methodist miner) disapproved of them.

When my mother and I reached Newcastle, I have no idea which shops we visited. But I do remember the fact that there was always a problem about me needing to go to the toilet. In the earlier years, before I started school, it seems that it was acceptable for small children to pee in a side street, shielded from public view by their mother's skirts. But by the time I was eight, I was being taken into a cubicle in the women's toilets while my mother waited outside the door. But on one occasion a woman saw me coming out and shouted at my mother, complaining that boys should not be in the women's toilets. My mother offered the defence that she was nervous of letting me go into the men's toilets unaccompanied. I had no idea why this was so, except that I had never actually been into men's public toilets before, and therefore would not have known about urinals. However, after that I was sent off into the proper place, and presumably I coped.

Green spaces make you happy is a commonly held belief, with quite a bit of research evidence to support it, although of course it depends on what you mean by green space, as well as what you mean by happy. It has become a normal part of urban planning to try to maintain areas of natural environment within, or accessible from, the concrete jungle. Even more interestingly, there is some research (Berman et al 2008) which suggests that there is also a cognitive or intellectual benefit in interacting with nature. People were found to perform better on tasks involving attention and memory after an hour's walk in an arboretum, compared with an hour's walk in the middle of town.

I am sure that I benefited from living in, or near, a green environment during my primary school years, compared with the alternative of staying in the streets of Consett town. However, did this generate extra disappointment later on when I had to move back to a concrete urban environment?

Ignoring risks (not worrying) was a behavioural possibility shown to me by that boy who encouraged my leap across the streaming river Derwent. Parents often focus on teaching their child to be aware of dangers, rather than how and when to ignore them, so this equally useful kind of knowledge might have to come from your more subversive peers. Ignoring things might look as if you are being blind to risks, and if that was true it would indeed be rather risky. More sensibly though, you would have considered the dangers but decided that it is safe to ignore them. This can be a delicate balance, of course. It would be stupid to ignore real problems, but equally you cannot get on with your life without ignoring risks from time to time. The most common risks in everyday life are fairly small ones, and it is perfectly reasonable to ignore them. Indeed, it is usually safer to give your full attention to the task in hand, rather than be distracted by thoughts about possible accidents.

It is very difficult to explain how to ignore things, and indeed doing nothing or not reacting can be the hardest thing to do. Surely once you have had a thought or worry, it isn't possible to undo it. This is indeed true, but ignoring something does not require it to vanish. It is still there, but you have decided not to make any response to it, at least for the moment. And if you are not going to respond to this thought, you might as well put it on hold.

5

UNHAPPY HOLIDAYS

1954

By the age of nine, I was well experienced in annual family holidays. My mother was always keen to *get away for a bit*, presumably to refresh herself from the daily and weekly grind of routine housework and childcare. My father was less keen, as he only had two weeks off work each year (this was the norm in those days), and he would have preferred to make use of this time for house maintenance, as well as his bee keeping.

We always went to the seaside, usually on the Northumberland, Durham or Yorkshire coasts, but once to Blackpool where I was shown the tower ballroom. *This is where that programme on the wireless comes from*, I was told by my mother, who was a great fan of Reginald Dixon and his Wurlitzer organ.

Another time there was a small caravan at Newbiggin, which is about 20 miles north of the Tyne. I hated caravans, having to cram yourself into the mean little space available, and in the morning having to trek across the cold wet grass and mud, on your way to the shower block. In those days most caravans did not have their own facilities, and you had to have a communal wash and go to the toilet in what appeared to be a wartime concrete bunker.

My holiday miseries were multiplied by the fact that I had a bed-wetting habit, which persisted intermittently until the age of eight or nine, causing embarrassment to my mother when she decided to try a holiday at a guest house in Whitby. Our holidays previously had been self-catering, so that she could take our own bed sheets and wash them as necessary. She felt obliged to take me to see the landlady when we arrived, to explain that I might have an accident in the night. For a moment the landlady hesitated, and I thought she was about to say that we would have to leave. But then she said not to worry, it would be all right. And fortunately I did not disgrace myself.

Another time, we went to the Butlins holiday camp at Filey. This had opened at the end of the War, and was very popular, with a capacity of many thousands. Apparently Billy Butlin's idea was to improve upon the holiday experience provided by the traditional seaside landlady, who ejected her guests from the premises first thing in the morning, not allowing them back in again until evening. However, my own feeling was that the holiday camp (which had been an army camp during the War) went to the other extreme and simply provided an alternative nightmare. I still remember the shock I felt on the first morning at breakfast. There was a dining room crammed full of tables as far as the eye could see (remember I was still a small boy), and there appeared to be identical families (two parents and two children) at each one. The noise was as huge as the number of people. In order to get through my breakfast (a rather tasteless porridge), I had to fight against a tremendous longing to be on my own, away from that place.

Going on holiday required my parents to do a lot of preparation during the preceding week. My father had to get the van ready, for example. As a plumber, he had a small van in which he transported his tools and materials. This was a rather faded red Singer vehicle probably of wartime vintage, with two seats in the front and room for two boxes in the back where my sister and I could sit or perch, next to the luggage. This part of the van was usually covered in a year's worth of dirty grease, so my father had to roll up his sleeves and get it cleaned out for our annual expedition.

Meanwhile, my mother would do all the packing. We did not have much in the way of clothes or possessions in those days, but if we were self-catering there would be a box full of foodstuffs, as well as bed sheets and towels. For some reason, my mother would get very tense over the packing, worrying in case she might have forgotten something. *We don't want to have to go and buy anything while we're there.* She had saved up hard to pay for the holiday, and had no spare money to waste. There was one occasion when it all came to a head. We were in the van and ready to set off, but then she suddenly wanted to take the suitcase back into the house to make sure she had packed everything. My father lost his temper: *I'm fed up with all this. I'm not going.* He left the van and went back in the house. My mother followed him in a bit of a panic, and then came back to tell us that he was sitting in his chair in a sulk. She would go and talk him round. *Don't worry*, she told us, although I don't recall that we were actually worried whether we went or not. Anyway, after a while my father came back and rather grimly started driving. It took him quite some time to cheer up.

Holidays were not really to my father's taste. He liked to be doing things, such as little jobs, gardening or looking after his bees. If he sat and did nothing, he fell asleep. Wandering aimlessly along the seafront with rain and wind coming off the North Sea was not his idea of pleasure. The only thing he liked doing on holiday was fishing, using a simple hook, line and sinker (no rod), swinging the line around his head and hurling it into the sea, from the end of the pier or off a suitable area of rocks. Then he could sit happily smoking his pipe while waiting for a fish to take the bait. In those days it was possible to catch a very edible fish by these simple means. This fish could be cooked by my mother if we were in a caravan, but otherwise it was presented to the landlady of the guest house, who would accept it gracefully and offer to cook it for us.

1955

Day trips to the seaside were much less fraught than a week's holiday, although the weather was always potentially hostile. One fine day at Whitley Bay we were sitting on the beach, my father wearing his Sunday suit and tie, as men did in those days even when the sun was shining. Suddenly the sky went dark and there was a lot of shouting. We looked round and saw a flood of water pouring off the promenade on to the beach and heading towards us and the sea. Then the cloudburst itself reached us, and we were being soaked from above while struggling to walk through deep flowing water coming down the beach. It was remarkably frightening, especially because of its suddenness. Eventually the small crowd of people reached the safety of the promenade and went to shelter in the doorway of a hotel. My mother opened the door and asked if we could come inside to shelter, but the hotel staff refused, causing her to mutter about the mean snobbishness of people in hotels. Fortunately the storm soon passed, so we gave up and went home to get dry.

There were some happier days, of course. The fine sandy beaches of Northumberland could be quite beautiful, even in the fog. I always enjoyed a trip to St. Mary's lighthouse at Whitley Bay, which is on an island but can be reached by a causeway at low tide. On one occasion my mother gave in to my wish to climb the spiral staircase up to the lantern room at the top, where we cringed at the height but admired the view.

And sometimes we went inland to Blanchland and Edmondbyers on the Durham moors. In July and August every year my father took his hives of bees up there to gather the heather honey, which is richer and more valuable than the lighter spring flower honey. On a Sunday afternoon we would take a trip out to the moors, so that he could check on his hives. Unfortunately, the roads around there can be quite steep, and there was one particular hill which always defeated our little old van. My father would put his foot down and try to get up this hill, but with four of us loaded into it, the van would slowly come to a halt somewhat short of the summit. So then we would have to get out and walk, allowing my father to coax the van up to the top. After that there would be a free-wheeling ride down the hill on the other side, to save petrol, and then my mother would scream at the increasing speed and get him to apply the brake.

Nocturnal enuresis (bed-wetting) used to be regarded by many psychiatrists as a sign of neurosis or stress in children. In fact this is true only for some cases of secondary enuresis, which is when the child (or even adult) starts bed wetting after having been dry. In primary enuresis, which is quite common even until the age of eight, the child is simply being a bit slow in developing the necessary physical maturity.

Two physical functions develop in children during their early years. The first is the production of antidiuretic hormone, which reduces the kidneys' output of urine at night. The second is the ability to sense a full bladder and then wake up. If a child is still bed wetting, an important part of the treatment is for the parent to avoid reacting with either anxiety or anger, because that could make it worse. It will almost certainly disappear of its own accord.

If some kind of treatment is to be tried (Brown, M.L. et al 2011), there may be some benefit in combining antidiuretic hormone therapy with a urine alarm under the bed sheets (a metal pad and battery powered alarm which is triggered by any wetness).

In my case, my bed wetting ceased entirely after starting a star chart (writing down each night as wet or dry, and being given points and a reward for any success). However, my improvement occurred almost instantly, so I think I must have simply reached physical maturity by that time.

Change is as good as a rest, they say. At least, both are (or can be) positive ways to reduce your general level of stress. Major changes or upheavals in your life are inevitable from time to time, for example bereavements, illnesses, house moves or new jobs, and of course these kinds of change are great generators of stress. But coping with them is surely more difficult if you are a person who always tries to avoid changes of any kind. So prepare yourself for change by deliberately unsettling your life a bit. Many everyday things can be done equally well in a number of different ways, so why stick to just one? For example vary the route you travel to work, or the place where you shop. Going on holiday to unfamiliar places provides a change of scene, as well as an upheaval of daily routine.

It is easier to cope with changes if you have volunteered for them, rather than being at their mercy. If you can see that certain changes are becoming inevitable, why not take the lead and bring them about yourself at a time of your choosing? For example, if you are in a failing marriage or bad relationship that has reached its breaking point, why wait for the other person to take the initiative? Some couples dither for a long time, each hoping that the other will take the blame for ending it, but this just creates more stress. Don't resist inevitable change. Go for it.

In the case of holidays, my mother was keen to go, to relieve the daily grind. But my father would have preferred to be at home (making a change from going to work), so he only went under protest and felt stressed by the whole business. In adulthood, I have followed my father in being disinclined to go on holidays. It is the luggage, queues and crowds which seem to get in the way.

6

THE ELEVEN-PLUS

1955

I took the eleven-plus exam, strangely, when I was ten. It was by no means the first time I had come across it, as our teacher was keen to give us special coaching every week during the year leading up to the real exam. She said that we needed to become familiar with the kind of questions that were being asked. Miss Wilson was a nice lady with clear ambitions for us all, although never pushing us further than we could go.

It was not from her, but from another boy, that I heard of the terrible importance of this exam. *If you don't pass, they send you to the secondary modern school. They are all rough lads there, always fighting.* If you wanted to get on in life, and avoid being beaten up by thugs, you really had to go to the grammar school. By this time I had decided that I wanted to be a scientist (unspecified), and clearly this would never happen if I failed the eleven-plus.

My sister had already passed the eleven-plus six years earlier, and was a pupil at Consett Grammar School. Indeed she was now old enough to leave and get a nice job in the bank. For a young woman from a working class family, this was a great success, and my mother expected me (as a boy) to do even better. I would be able to get a *good job,* certainly better than my father, who was merely a plumber. She promised me an incentive for passing the exam, but I cannot remember what it was. I imagine it was some money. The other children at school compared notes on what they had been promised: *I'm going to get a bike. I'm going to get a watch.*

The big day finally arrived, and I had to find my way to the exam room at Consett Grammar School. Later, when the exam was over, school dinners were provided. This was a new experience for me, and I particularly remember enjoying the bowl of figs and custard for pudding. I remember it because my mother asked me what we had had, and this made her laugh. She was thinking of the Syrup of Figs that she gave me from time to time, to make sure that my bowels were in working order.

A couple of months later a letter arrived to say that I had passed the exam. I was of course much relieved, especially as I had completed the exam paper with lots of time to spare, and had sat there wondering if I had got it all wrong. I still remembered the teacher at infants' school telling me off for completing a task too quickly.

At school some weeks later, Miss Wilson checked whether we had all received our results through the post. We had been sent a strange letter in which the education authority offered us a place at the grammar school, and we had to say whether we wanted to take up this offer or would rather go to the secondary modern school. Did anyone actually turn it down, I wonder. Anyway, it turned out that five children in the class had not passed the exam. Miss Wilson gathered them together to commiserate, and to try to persuade them that their life had not come to an end. She did not sound terribly convincing. Some of them started crying, and I looked at them with horror, as if they had been sentenced to hang. It was only years later that I realised that the proportion of pupils generally who went to grammar school was quite small (a fifth at most), and therefore it was surprising that only five children in my class had failed the exam. Presumably the classes had been carefully streamed, and in addition we had received some advantage from all that special coaching.

We still had some time to wait for our new lives. This was the spring, and we would not start Grammar School until the autumn. There was time to consider the end of childhood and the beginning of the march towards adulthood. This was not entirely a joyous prospect, leading as it did towards work and then death. I was beginning to have bad feelings about the future. One day Miss Wilson had been talking about the year 2000. This seemed extremely remote, like something out of science fiction, and I asked her whether we would still be alive in the year 2000. Patiently, she got me to do the elementary arithmetic which showed that I would be 55 then, and therefore likely to be still here. So at least I could afford to forget about death for the time being. But there was still the issue of work. When Miss Wilson asked me one day whether I was looking forward to growing up, I said no, because then I would have to go to work. Despite all my high-flown ideas about becoming a scientist, I could not believe that real life would allow me to be any different to my father.

The Tripartite System of education was established by the 1944 Butler Education Act. There would be grammar schools, secondary modern schools and technical schools, with pupils being selected on the basis of their particular aptitudes at age 11. In practice, technical school places were insufficient, and it all became a fierce competition for places at the prestigious grammar schools, who received an unfair allocation of resources. Many secondary modern schools started to acquire the reputation of being sink schools. This system fell into disrepute because it gave an advantage to middle class boys living in particular areas, and also because of doubts over the accuracy of the testing procedure.

Having said all that, some positive things were achieved by the eleven-plus exam (Wooldridge 1995). Before this, working class children had very little chance of receiving more than the most elementary schooling. The eleven-plus exam proved finally that many of these children had great ability and could benefit from an advanced level of education. The problem was that this was just a first step, which formed a new elite but neglected the idea of universal education for the less academic. By 1976 schools were moving towards a more comprehensive system, with children of all abilities within one school, although they would still be in classes that were streamed in various ways.

IQ tests in general have fallen into popular disrepute because of these issues. How can they not be unfair if you say that someone with a score of 115 is a pass and someone scoring 114 is a failure? Especially if the error of measurement is give or take 10.

The earlier eleven-plus tests contained some questions which were clearly biased towards middle class children, and a lot of technical work was done to try to make it measure a pure IQ. However, it can only ever be an approximation, especially when it is obtained from a single paper-and-pencil test done on a mass basis (rather than individually administered tests, although these too have their limitations). Having said all that, IQ tests are still more accurate on average than many other ways of assessing people that we use every day.

Social mobility is considerably affected by education, which is why some parents today are still making extraordinary efforts to get their children into the best school. My own upward ascent had now started after passing the eleven-plus. I am grateful for the opportunities which I gained from this piece of social engineering, although of course there would be a price to be paid.

A good job is important in life, but not necessarily in the way that my mother expressed it. She was referring to money and social status, but these are not always good indicators of job satisfaction (although often quite important).

A job should fit your particular strengths and weaknesses. You have to be brutally honest with yourself about these. You should be able to take some decisions and have some control over what you do. Never think that you just have to do what you are told. This is seldom true even when it appears to be so. Your work should be absorbing, so that time passes quickly. This tends to be when the work is challenging but not overwhelming. You should be able to further develop your skills. This will give you an opportunity either to move to a better job, or to improve the present one.

You should have opportunities for interpersonal contact and friendships at work. Although some people prefer not to socialise with colleagues, you can still gain valuable support from everyday conversations with them.

Ideally you should not have to uproot yourself from family or friends in order to move to another area. If you do have to move, make sure that you are prepared to accept the loss of these connections. I later found myself moving away from my home area, and indeed was keen to so. At the same time, I am now quite sad about that. Most children who passed the eleven-plus did not move south, and remained of benefit to the North-East.

7

GATESHEAD

1955

When I was still just ten years old, my father surprised me by asking if I might want to go into the family plumbing business when I was a bit older. My mother frowned upon him asking such a question: *He seems to think it's the same as when he left school at the age of 12 to go and work for his father.* Maybe grandad had suggested it. The business consisted of just the two of them now, with my father doing nearly all the plumbing, while his elderly father dealt mainly with the office work and money. Grandad had reached an age when he wanted to retire, but my father felt incapable of taking over and *doing the books.* He had no confidence with arithmetic and writing, but maybe I could start doing some of the paperwork until I was old enough to leave school and join the business. *Could you see yourself becoming a plumber?* He knew the answer to this, really, and I could tell that he simply felt obliged to ask.

My mother had often drummed it into me that I must not even consider becoming a plumber. *It's an awful dirty job, and your da gets barely enough money to live on.* She didn't need to tell me, really. Joining pipes together never looked very interesting, however skilled it might be. I wanted to be some kind of scientist, although I kept this to myself. They would have laughed at this childishly unrealistic idea.

All I could say was I did not wish to become a plumber, even if this meant that grandad would have to close the business. I felt a degree of guilt about letting my father down, but also knew that my mother would be glad to see him escape from grandad (the *mean ould devil*). This was a sad moment in the long history of A. R. Smith and Son, Plumbers and Gasfitters, of Sherburn Terrace, Consett. In the early 1800s, the original Smiths were a family of shoemakers in Tynemouth, until one of them moved to Consett as a plumber in the 1870s. He was succeeded by two of his sons, John and Alec (my grandad). Eventually only Alec and my father were left, until they shut up shop in 1956.

So my father had to start looking for new employment. Out of loyalty to the family history, he refused an offer from a rival family of plumbers in Consett, and instead opted for a job with Gateshead Council. This was about fifteen miles away, so the decision was made to move house to Gateshead.

1956

Despite regular shopping trips to Newcastle with my mother, I had never been into Gateshead before. It was very much the poor relation of Newcastle, without the big shops and splendid buildings that attracted people over the bridge to the superior side of the river. My parents told me that they had found quite a nice house on the outskirts of Gateshead, and I would be able to go to the Grammar School there.

On moving day we packed ourselves into my father's old van, and after a slow journey to Gateshead we found Old Durham Road, continued through Deckham and Carr Hill, and finally climbed towards Sheriff Hill. When I look at this route on Google Street View today, it does not look too bad at all, and perhaps it has been improved over the years. I still remember my heart sinking as I sat in the back of the van, looking at the grim or derelict buildings, with not a blade of grass to be seen. And then I put my foot in it. I just had to say what I was thinking: *I'm glad we're not going to live just here, it looks terrible.* There was a great hesitation in the van as they tried to think how to tell me that we were going to live not too far from here. Sensing that I had said the wrong thing, I did a very quick U-turn: *But this part here looks better.* I was lying, but then realised that it was actually fairly true.

We turned into Egremont Drive, and it was not too bad at all. A quirky house with a flat roof and battlements *like a castle!* And there was an area of grass and trees in the middle of the circle of houses. Over the wall behind the house there was a vast storage yard, six feet deep in broken glass, extending over an acre or so. *At least it's clean rubbish*, joked my mother. Later on I would enjoy dark nights looking out of my bedroom window at the light of the moon reflecting wonderfully on this sea of broken glass. Also I would enjoy playing cricket with some local lads in the little park at the front. Later on I would be intrigued by the sound of a rock band playing in the house at the end of the Drive. The fish shop at the end of the street was owned by the Steel family, and John Steel would become the drummer with the Animals.

At first, however, I was not sure what to make of Gateshead. I had no idea where I was or what I was going to do, but clearly there was no choice about being here. I was going to have to knuckle down and make the best of it. We would hardly ever visit Consett or my river Derwent again.

The stress of moving house is well known to adults, if only because of all the perils and annoyances in the process of selling and buying houses. Psychological research has also supported the idea that moving house can take its toll on children (Oishi and Schimmack 2010). Uprooting to new surroundings at an early age can cause stress, the effects of which can stretch into adulthood. Possible ill-effects include lower life satisfaction, lower psychological well-being, and fewer quality social relationships. People who are introverted are affected more than extraverts in terms of their social relationships, presumably because they have more difficulty in starting new friendships after moving.

The average number of moves during childhood in this survey (in the USA) was just two, suggesting that three or more moves start to become risky. However, this obviously depends on the sort of move, the reason for it, and how many changes are involved, not to mention all the other individual stress factors which will be different from person to person.

It is doubtful whether people would be able to calculate all of the unknown risks (and benefits) of a move before having made it. However, at least they should pay due consideration to all these aspects, and ask themselves whether a move is really necessary, or whether there are ways of minimising the risks.

In the case of my family's move to Gateshead, it is possible to say that it was not strictly necessary. My father could have swallowed his pride and taken another job in Consett. But he and my mother could see the advantages of a job with the council, a job which would be secure and with a pension (unlike the uncertainties of being a one-man business). And there would be more opportunities for me and my sister in the big city environment of Gateshead and Newcastle. The big city might look rather frightening, but it would do me good to get used to it.

Perhaps it was my mother who would gain the least, and suffer the most, from this move. As a middle-aged non-working woman in an unfamiliar town, she had no easy way of making new social contacts.

Lying is usually considered part of the dark side of human nature. Everyone is familiar with the hurt that results from being deceived or lied to, and therefore it is almost universally frowned upon. Most people can see that society would become impossible if each of us did not stick to the truth as far as we know it, as often as we can. And therefore we are shocked by occasional individuals who seem to have no basic regard for the truth (Psychopathic or Machiavellian personality disorders). However, such a persistent part of human nature is likely to have served some function in maintaining our survival. It must have a good side.

To lie simply means to present to the world something other than your actual thoughts or feelings. You might give a picture that is incorrect, or you might just keep it all to yourself and hide the fact that there is anything to tell. This could serve various justifiable purposes. For example you could be defending yourself against someone's unreasonable intrusion into your privacy. Or you might be smoothing over an awkward situation where the truth would do more harm than good. For example, when saying no to someone's demands you might use some polite fiction, saving face for the other person. If you want to turn down an invitation to a boring party, you can avoid insulting the host and his friends by saying you are already booked to go somewhere else. This is a situation where no one really wants to know the truth, and therefore your dishonesty is quite safe.

When I cringed and said that Sheriff Hill did not look too bad, I was telling a diplomatic lie. But it also expressed a truth, namely that I was content to accept this place as my new home. I would get used to it.

8

THE GRAMMAR SCHOOL

1956

At the age of eleven I was still in short trousers, as was the norm in those days, but now there was a grammar school blazer to wear over a formal shirt and tie. There was even a schoolboy cap, but this tended to fall off or get mocked by secondary modern school children, so most boys did not wear it. There were no girls, after the building of a new Grammar School for Girls in another part of town. The blazer was maroon in colour, with the school badge on the breast pocket. On the badge was a picture of a goat's head (*Gateshead – get it?*), with the motto Toil No Soil (see this at the Gateshead Grammar School website). Strangely, no one could work out the meaning of the motto, although teachers tried to persuade us that it meant *Work is no disgrace.* Some boys joked that it was advising us not to become gardeners.

I soon learned the various possible routes between home and school. There were frequent buses up and down Old Durham Road, and my mother gave me the bus fare. However, she said I could keep the fare if I walked. This was only a few pennies, but it added up each week. Apart from that she gave me no regular pocket money, so it was quite important to save the bus fares. However, I soon discovered that Old Durham Road did not make a pleasant walk, especially uphill on the steep final stretch at Sheriff Hill. On the way home at 4pm there were always convoys of school buses slowly climbing the hill packed with lads and lasses. These were the secondary school pupils, those who had failed the eleven-plus, and they seemed to have something against the likes of me. The lads would hang their faces out of the top of the bus windows, shouting *Grammar School Snob* at the sight of my school blazer and my satchel full of books and homework. They had none of these things.

So instead of walking the main road, I found a much nicer walk through the side streets. From the school gates in Prince Consort Road, I crossed Durham Road and then off up Dryden Road. Then there were several streets until some steep steps led up to the bottom end of Egremont Drive. This was a quiet one-mile walk with virtually no traffic (only a minority of people owned cars at that time), and soon I knew every inch of it.

1957

During my first week at the grammar school, I had noticed something was wrong. The rest of the class appeared to be not particularly clever, which was not what I expected after all this strict selection by IQ test. The teacher was struggling with their lack of simple arithmetic or elementary geometry. Miss Wilson would have been very disappointed with them. I felt as if my education had ground to a halt, and this was quite depressing. But then a lad in the playground explained that there were four classes in the first year, and that I was in the bottom class. They had been streamed according to their eleven-plus results.

I could not understand this. At Consett I had been told that my score was very high, so I wondered if there had been some kind of mix-up. *Why have I been put in the bottom class?* I asked a friendly-looking teacher. He explained that because I had taken the eleven-plus in the Consett area, the exam and the marking might have been different to here in Gateshead. And Consett had not actually disclosed my marks, so I was being started off in the low stream to be on the safe side. *But don't worry, you'll take the school exams at the end of term, and we'll sort you into the right class then.* Up until then I had been keeping my head down in the class, trying not to stand out as too clever, but now I realised that I would have to fight for position, otherwise I might be in the bottom class for ever. *I'll show them.*

In the end-of-term exams, I scored the highest marks in the whole of the first year, way above anyone in the bottom class, and I was moved instantly to the top class. This was very pleasing, but it now meant that I had a position to maintain. The school encouraged this competitiveness by means of a yearly ritual, when each teacher read out the exam results, giving each pupil a rank in his class. If you were middle ranking, this was a comfortable position, as you could go up or down from year to year without anyone remembering or noticing. Whereas if you were top of the class, as I was, a great deal of attention was given to the possibility that you might be beaten into second place. I would spend a lot of time over the following years doing extra home study, in order to stay at the top.

During the first two years at grammar school we had to learn Latin. But perhaps we were unable to hide our lack of interest in this subject, and to relieve our boredom the Latin teacher had a regular habit of punishing at least two pupils during every class, using the edge of a wooden ruler to hit their knuckles. Sometimes blood was drawn. One time he decided to punish the entire front row of the class, including myself. It really hurt, although I pretended that it did not. I have no idea what I had done to offend him.

Eventually this teacher disappeared from the school, amid the rumour that a pupil had told his parents, leading to a complaint being laid. Most of us had no idea that a teacher's behaviour could be challenged.

1958

Aged thirteen now, a new teenager, I was heading rapidly

towards being six feet tall. It was embarrassing to be still wearing short trousers, so I told my mother that *everyone else has got long trousers.* Some months later, when studying the school photograph, she spotted the fact that half the class still had short trousers, but by that time I had got what I wanted. She took me into a shop in Newcastle for some grey flannels, and the salesman grinned at me: *Your first pair, are they?* It was a big deal for a boy in those days. Actually it was quite uncomfortable to wear these long trousers at first, especially as they were rather baggy and a bit too long. My mother always said I would *grow into* any new clothes she bought for me.

I couldn't entirely escape the embarrassment of showing my legs, however, as the school was keen that we should take regular vigorous exercise, and this required the wearing of a thin white vest and matching cotton shorts. The PE teacher led the class on a run through the neighbouring park and then back along the streets to the school. People looked at us with some amusement, but we didn't mind too much as we all looked pitiful together. This was in the cold winter of the North-East, when scantily clad adult runners were rarely seen. By the time we were heading back towards the school, the class had strung itself out, with the sporty muscular lads in the lead, and the thin or fat lads trailing behind. I was one of the thin ones, and actually could have run faster, but I took pity on a friend who was rather fat and could not keep up. So I always came in last alongside him. He was a good excuse not to be competitive, for once.

Competitiveness *is a marked feature of many forms and fields of education, especially those who would describe themselves as seeking excellence. Schools strive for greater examination success, and university academics compete to have a greater number of publications. Some people say that competition between schoolchildren* is good, because it builds character and produces excellence. Others dislike the extremes to which competitiveness can go, but concede that in moderation it can be healthy and fun.

But there is also a view that competition is inherently destructive, unnecessary and inappropriate at school (Alfie Kohn 1993). This is not to say that children shouldn't learn discipline and tenacity, and that they shouldn't be encouraged to succeed. None of these require a child to aim to beat other children or worry about being beaten. Competition often makes children anxious, and that interferes with concentration. It is more effective and more realistic for a child to measure his performance against himself to see if he is improving over time.

There is also a risk that trying to be Top will take precedence over more meaningful reasons for learning something. In my case I concentrated more and more on mathematics, because I found this the easiest way of getting high marks. It simply required lots of hours on my own with paper and a pencil and a few books. But years later I would lose all real interest in mathematics, and to that extent my effort was wasted.

Striving is a way of acquiring resources or achieving aims. You work hard specifically to achieve your goal, rather than waiting for it to drop into your lap (although this also can sometimes get results). Working towards something, trying to make things happen, might seem to be the more reliable method. However, you can take this too far, becoming over-conscientious and trying to achieve too much at too high a standard. There are times when it is better to be satisfied with good enough, or even to wait for someone else to do things for you.

When you see a high-achieving person demonstrating their expertise (for example a concert pianist), it is tempting to believe that they have some special ability that you could never acquire. In fact they have made themselves special through the amount and type of effort that they have put into it. Even if they do have some special inborn talent, this would have been just the beginning.

Skills fade with lack of practice. This applies even to everyday skills such as reading, writing and arithmetic, which can become somewhat rusty if you don't do them much. Refresh your skills from time to time. You never know when you might need them.

But at grammar school I focussed too much on achieving exam results that proved to be a waste of time. That wasn't just me being silly. It was what the system expected.

9

MONEY AND CLASS

1958

Gateshead Grammar School was not really a posh school, except in the eyes of the secondary modern crowd. Anyone properly posh would have gone to the private Royal Grammar School in Newcastle. At the time of the eleven-plus Miss Wilson had offered me the chance of taking the entrance exams for a free scholarship to the RGS, but I refused. Even at that age I knew my place.

My social elevation to the state grammar school was quite sufficient to be going on with. I gathered that most of my classmates had fathers who worked in offices, and one was a doctor, but they never talked about money or what sort of houses they had. But they did look at me rather curiously when I confessed that my father was a plumber. Of course, this might have been due to my own visible shame in admitting to such a father. My mother had made it clear to me that plumbing was a dirty job, a lowly job. It wasn't even clean dirt, like the coal dust that her father had suffered as a miner. Miners had showers, made good money, and earned respect. Plumbers groped about in other people's waste products.

At least four other lads in my class must have been working class, as they always put up their hands for free school dinners. This was a means-tested benefit, and the teacher tended to speak in hushed tones when asking for their hands to be raised, while the rest of the class pretended to take no notice. I avoided this shame by never having school dinners, and always going home for a snack such as beans on toast.

Gateshead Grammar School had the usual traditional social class-related features. As well as the Latin teaching and associated punishments mentioned earlier, sports lessons involved rugby rather than football, English required the memorisation of Shakespeare, and music was classical in style.

One day, the music teacher asked for volunteers to start a school orchestra. *Can anyone play the violin?* Strangely enough, I could. At primary school there had been a peripatetic music teacher, who came weekly and gave us lessons on the violin. At first we had been given the loan of child-sized instruments, and then my mother was persuaded to buy me a cheap full-sized one. I hadn't actually touched it since leaving primary school, and might not have volunteered to start again, but the music teacher said I could play in the orchestra instead of attending the singing class. I had always said that I could not sing, and even the teacher who once told me that *anyone can sing, they just think they can't*, had given me up as a bad job. So I would rather scrape away on a violin than make a fool of myself with my voice.

This was yet another task to practise at home, of course. I was quite content to do things on my own, not only school work but also various hobbies such as making model aeroplanes and collecting postage stamps. I became quite obsessed with getting the violin to sound right, something that requires many hours of work over a number of years. The violin, in its black wooden case, had to be carried between home and school at least once per week, and I had to try to ignore my embarrassment at being seen with it. It was something else, along with my blazer and satchel full of books, marking me out as a *grammar school snob*.

A new boy arrived at the school, explaining that his family had moved to the area because of his father's job. He was a nice lad, as smiley as I was, but everyone laughed at him because he spoke with a posh accent. He came from *down south*, the Home Counties, somewhere near London. The only other people we had heard speaking like this were BBC announcers and the Queen. When he said that he could not quite understand some of the things we said, I was really puzzled. My mother had always said that our family did not have strong Geordie accents, as we came from County Durham, whereas lower class Tynesiders had much harsher accents and a lot of dialect. But this was before we had tape recorders, and in fact I had no idea how I sounded.

This was my first glimmer of insight into having a Geordie accent, and how the rest of the world might see it. One day the English teacher gave us another pause for thought. He asked us to read out loud and try to imitate a BBC accent. When I attempted this, it was quite excruciating, and everyone fell about laughing. Quite simple things were surprisingly hard. The teacher suggested that we should say *yes* instead of *aye* in our normal conversation, and even this simple thing proved to be incredibly difficult. Saying *yes* felt agonisingly posh, and it stuck in the throat.

Fortunately the lad from the South was friendly enough to the natives, and from him I learned that being posh and wealthy was not necessarily a bad thing. He showed me where he lived, an impressive house with a garden and even a small wood. Outside was parked an expensive-looking car, and he asked me if I knew what sort it was. I read out the name on the back: Armstrong Siddeley. *It's an Armstrong Siddeley Sapphire Automatic*, he corrected me. *My father's very proud of it.*

I'm not sure if his mother really approved of him having me as a friend, and this might have been reinforced by the occasion when I ventured to call at his house unannounced, and asked her *Is Jimmy coming out to play?* She looked at me curiously: *You mean David?* The problem here was that someone at school had nicknamed him Jimmy, his surname being Riddle, and this had stuck so well that we had actually forgotten his proper name. I had absolutely no idea that *Jimmy Riddle* was a slang term for urination (rhyming with piddle). I also have no idea whether his mother understood this. She kept a very straight face.

Speaking Geordie (or any other regional accent) can have a significant influence on a person's life, because of the stigma that may be attached to it amongst other sections of society. In modern times, the more extreme forms of the Tyneside accent, coming from specific localities, have tended to level out into a more general north-eastern brand of English (Watt, D. 2002). Nevertheless, it remains very distinctive, and is still potentially handicapping in terms of intelligibility and perceived social class.

A person with this accent can be quite ambivalent about it. On the one hand there is a sense of regional pride, and a disdain towards soft southerners. But on the other hand there can be an awareness of the prejudice that might be suffered at the hands of these southerners, the people who have most of the money and power in the country.

Even today, when Geordie accents have become fairly familiar to the rest of the country through a number of people who appear on television, the accent may be regarded as comical although pleasant and friendly. Someone who wishes to develop a professional career might well consider moderating it as much as possible. However, fifty years ago the situation was much worse. An unadulterated Tyneside accent would have caused the speaker to be regarded as a low class foreigner, especially in the south. When I eventually left the North-East to attend University, I went to the trouble of practising my speech with a tape recorder, to try to soften its edges and not draw attention to myself. Even now, after living away from the North-East for forty years, it can still feel as if I am in a foreign land!

Introversion is a personality trait, but sometimes it can feel like another kind of social class which separates you from other people. But despite what extraverts might say, it is not abnormal or peculiar. What is wrong with liking your own company? Having said that, introverts do need to have some degree of social contact with others, and if they are deprived of this for any length of time they feel isolated, lonely or uneasy, leading to emotional numbing and depression. Introverted people might seem to have a less outgoing life in terms of quantity of socialising, but the more important difference lies in their preferred type of social contact. Introverts cannot understand the foolishness of those who love going out to parties or restaurants where everyone is shouting to be heard. For them, an enjoyable conversation requires peace and quiet, one to one or in a very small group. In contrast, extraverts simply enjoy the buzz of a crowd.

By the time I became a teenager, it was clear that I was an introverted personality, being quite happy to spend time on my own, whether studying or entertaining myself. In this, I had followed both my father and mother. My friends were fairly few, partly due to the move away to Gateshead, cutting all previous ties, but compounded by the fact that I was never particularly desperate for company.

I wish I had been able to sing at school. It would have involved a great deal less work and stress than learning to play the violin. Maybe my introversion got in the way, making me too shy to make sounds from my throat, but it is also the case that some people really cannot sing (in tune), despite their best efforts, and they miss out on its benefits. Singing has physical effects such as improving breathing skills, while psychologically there is a lifting of mood. Socially, people feel good while singing in groups, and this can help to form bonds between them. Although playing the violin in the school orchestra did give me some opportunities for extraverted performances, it also required much lonely practice to reach exacting standards. It was a much more stress-provoking activity.

More generally, introverts can feel as if they belong to an inferior social class, not belonging to any of the usual crowds. To a teenager it becomes painfully obvious that other people are much better at joining in with things, whereas you hold back. It is hard not to start wondering what is wrong with you. All of the people that you would like to follow seem to be socially confident extraverts, so how could you ever become like them? Eventually of course you have to learn that the confidence of extraversion is a great illusion, and introversion can be a much more secure position. But a teenager would not know this.

10

DON'T BE LIKE YOUR DA

1958

My mother nagged, criticised, blamed and belittled my father all the time, for many years, as long as I can remember. She did it to his face, and she did it behind his back, with me as her audience. She had a powerfully convincing tone of voice, and there was a degree of truth in what she said, so it never occurred to me to question her statements. She also gave an explanation for the way she launched her attack daily and repeatedly: *You have to keep on nagging him, to get him to do anything.* My father hardly ever argued back, most of the time just shrugging it off. But occasionally a state of desperation must have built up in him, and out loud he *wished he was dead*, for which he would get another telling off. She accused him of upsetting me by saying such things, and indeed his combination of misery and anger was quite worrying.

What a sight he looks, she used to say to me. He would arrive home from work in his dungaree-type overalls, which would have acquired a great variety of dubious stains during the day. And then she would start washing them, not an easy task in the days before washing machines. They had to be soaked and scrubbed, rinsed and put through a mangle. Drying wasn't easy either, sometimes taking several days in the cold weather, draped over a clothes horse in front of the fire. My mother had been doing this chore over and over again for many years, and no doubt she was sick of it. But she blamed my father for making it worse: *If he took more care he would get less dirt on him.*

What a dirty face! Can you not get washed, man? This was another regular complaint. My father tended not to shave in the morning, to save time in the cold early morning rush. So by the time he arrived home in the evening, a growth of dark stubble would have developed on his face. Just imagine him in his dirty overalls, carrying his oily canvas bag of plumber's tools over his shoulder, and then imagine my mother saying *For goodness sake, man, you look like a tramp. I don't know what people will think, seeing you looking like that.*

It is not unusual for teenagers to be self-conscious about being seen in public with their parents, for all sorts of reasons. But there was one occasion when I was coming home from school, walking up the hill, and suddenly I caught up with my father coming home early from work. He had walked from his last job of the day, and was struggling slowly up the hill with his bag of tools on his back. There I was in my grammar school outfit, and there he was *looking like a tramp*. It occurred to me that people would be looking at me and then at him, *and what would they think?* I had an urge to run, and with the words *Sorry, can I hurry on, I've got things to do,* I left him behind and rushed home. At the same time, I felt a terrible guilt about being ashamed of my father, and when I got home I hid in my room rather than face him. But maybe he thought nothing of it. Or maybe he too felt happier walking alone.

What a smell he makes was another of my mother's regular sayings. My father enjoyed a variety of smoky activities, and my mother objected to them all. There were his bonfires at the allotment, when he would lean on his spade, completely enveloped in a swirling cloud of smoke, and when he came home for tea the bonfire smell came with him. *Can you not keep out of the smoke, man? It's all over your overalls, and then I have to wash them.*

Another sore point was his bee keeping. This involved using a smoker, a hand-held metal box with a nozzle at the front and bellows at the rear. Inside the box, old rags were set alight to smoulder, so that smoke would puff out of the nozzle when the bellows were squeezed. By puffing smoke over the bees in the hive, they would be pacified and less likely to sting. But it annoyed my mother when she smelled it on his overalls. *What on earth have you been burning now, man?*

However, the most frequent source of smoke was the tobacco in his pipe. This was filled with strong *baccy* sliced off a solid lump of Condor Bar, which he kept in a small tin. Like most men in those days, he had smoked since his early teens, and preferred the really strong stuff. There was no awareness of the health hazards at that time, and the only objection my mother could come up with was the fact that it was an unpleasant smell that made her cough. They did not know then that he would get throat cancer at the age of 70, followed by stomach cancer at the age of 80.

It was quite true that his pipe did produce an impressively noxious smell. The clouds of smoke would form a thick choking fog in any room where he was sitting, so he was allowed to smoke only in the back kitchen, the room closest to the outside door. Preferably, he was encouraged to go to his shed, where he kept warm with an oil heater. My mother tried once to get him to buy a scented tobacco, like our white-collar neighbour who worked in an office and did his gardening in what looked like his best pullover. But my father found this type of tobacco to be weak and unsatisfying.

At one time he was very short of money, and tried to make his own smokes by using *poor man's baccy* (coltsfoot) which someone had told him about. We had an afternoon in the country, picking it from around the edge of the fields. The leaves took a long time to dry, and in his pipe they produced a smell very much like an autumn bonfire. There was no real content of course, no nicotine, and he endured this for only a week before returning with relief to his normal tobacco.

What a noise he makes was yet another daily complaint. These noises all came out of my father's mouth. During the day there were his eating habits, and at night there was his snoring. He did indeed eat noisily, chewing at length and apparently in vain, while making smacking noises with his cheeks. Then he would take a slurp of hot milky tea into his mouth, to try to lubricate the process. It might have been due to ill-fitting dentures, of course. Like many people in the 1920's, he had had all his teeth extracted when he was eighteen, because of the prevailing pseudo-scientific view (focal infection theory) that this would prevent the occurrence of all sorts of common diseases.

My mother also had false teeth, but ate silently. She kept nagging him to *try to eat more quietly, man,* with some limited success. However, she had no choice but to accept that being a snorer was not his fault, and all she could say was *try not to sleep on your back, man.* It cannot be denied that his snoring was a huge and penetrating noise, which even the neighbours once mentioned. Not having a spare bedroom, my mother was reduced to having twin beds and poking him with a broom handle when she couldn't sleep.

Whenever my mother and I were on our own, perhaps short of better things to talk about, she would launch into these complaints about my father. It was always *I don't know what people must think of him.* The lesson for me was *don't be like your da.* And most importantly, *what would people think?* She was having no success in changing my father, as he simply ignored what she said and kept his thoughts to himself. But I might be more amenable. Like any other teenager, I would not want to risk the derision of other people.

Exposure to inter-parental conflict *is commonly assumed to be distressing for a child, and possibly a source of psychological or behavioural problems either at the time or later on. However, the situation is highly complex, starting with the question of what actually constitutes inter-parental conflict, and how frequent or intense it needs to be to have any significant effect. Nagging, complaining, arguing and even violence between parents, may be witnessed directly by the child. Or it might go on out of earshot, but still leading to an atmosphere which is sensed by the child. And there are other more subtle ways of expressing conflict, such as avoidance and stonewalling, which need to be included in the equation.*

When careful research is done (not an easy task), it is not always clear whether inter-parental conflict does cause problems in the child, at least as a simple universal rule. The effects are much more complex, and depend on psychological processes within the individual child (Shelton and Harold 2008). For example, does the child actually see it as worrying, and does he blame himself for any of it? And then how does the child try to cope with the conflict? For example, he might try to mediate neutrally between his parents to stop the conflict. Or he might take sides and get involved in the argument. Another strategy might be to avoid and walk away from the conflict. Or to pretend that it doesn't bother him.

In my case, I dealt with the conflict by taking my mother's side, as did my sister. This presumably helped my mother by supporting her in her worries and irritations about my father, while he appeared not to need any support. It all went over his head. But what would happen if I ever came to see this as rather one-sided?

Another question is why was my mother so persistently denigrating about my father? Was this a prolonged bad mood brought on by the menopause, for example, or by sleep deprivation due to his snoring? Was it the end result of years of stress from the Second World War, marriage, children and money worries? Or was it just a nasty streak in her life-long personality? It could have been all of those. She went on nagging at my father until his death.

A further question is whether our support served only to make her worse. After I (and my sister) had absorbed the view that my father deserved to be denigrated, she was certainly never seriously challenged.

The power of words should not be underestimated, especially in the case of children or teenagers who have not yet learned how to see through them. We use words to represent reality, and therefore they can have a surprisingly real effect on you, for good or ill.

You have to learn to protect yourself from the effect of toxic words. In amongst all the good stuff that you listen to, there is also a lot of rubbish, and some of this can do damage. Most rubbish originates from ignorance rather than malice, but from time to time you will come across people who say things deliberately to cause you harm. They try to wind you up by saying things that are very worrying or anger-provoking. Or they may tell lies in order to manipulate you to their advantage.

If you do not know whether someone is entirely trustworthy or reliably accurate, it is wise to apply a certain amount of cynicism or humour when listening to them. You do not have to show this openly, of course, otherwise you might offend someone who is actually being genuine. Just keep an open mind or reserve your judgement. Check their words against reality.

However, it is doubtful whether I could have done anything to avoid the effects of listening to my mother, when she was denigrating my father repeatedly over all those years. I would have been an unusually wise child. Perhaps my father should have helped by challenging her views, rather than being passive and saying nothing. But of course he was just coping for himself in the only way that he knew.

Or perhaps I could have talked to someone about it. But I don't know if I would have done so (my mother once told me to keep my mouth shut about our family business, I cannot recall why). And who would have listened or realised its significance?

Or perhaps I should have been smarter in interpreting what she said, understanding that she was simply expressing her own worries, and that these represented fears rather than reality. But I was a child, and had no idea about such things. Is there any child who does?

This illustrates the fact that it is simply not possible to prevent all possibility of psychological problems. The world has a nasty tendency to inflict damage upon us when we are least prepared for it. That is why we need resilience, or a recovery plan, to undo any damage.

11

HE'S FALLEN OFF A LADDER

1959

My father seemed quite stoical in various situations that might have bothered other people. Perhaps sucking on his pipe helped him turn a deaf ear to my mother's nagging, for example. In contrast, my mother had an assortment of minor phobias of things such as having mice in the house, or being stung by insects such as bees. She thought him a *silly old fool* when he came back from his beehives with his arms swollen from too many stings. In those days bee keepers did not dress in all the protective clothing that they wear today, and he only wore a veil over his cap and face. He tried to tell my mother that bee stings were good for his arthritis, but she was worried that too many stings at one time might make him ill and even put him in hospital. *How would we manage for money if he was off work?*

But then one day disaster did strike. *Your da's had an accident*, my mother told me when I arrived home from school. Her voice was hushed, and for a moment I thought he must be dead. It emerged that he wasn't dead, but easily could have been. The idea of climbing ladders was something else that frightened my mother but was just part of a plumber's job. He had been working up a ladder, mending a gutter, and he or the ladder had slipped. His spine had been fractured, which to me sounded like a death sentence. When I had read stories about people breaking their backs, they always died. My mother looked very grim but calm. She would wait and see. I went very quiet for the rest of the afternoon.

After visiting him in hospital that evening, my mother came back restored and with her voice no longer hushed. *It was his own fault, the silly old fool,* she had established. She was a great reader of detective novels, and occasionally in real life she would get an opportunity to interrogate someone about some small misdemeanour, ending with a triumphant exposure of the guilty party. In his hospital bed, it is possible that my father had confessed immediately rather than face interrogation, knowing that she would blame him anyway. *It was because he lost his temper,* she reported to me, referring to another of my father's bad habits that I should try not to follow. Quite often when he was doing some repair job at home, he would get very irritated, especially if the job was proving to be awkward (as plumbing often is). Then he might swear and throw his tools to the floor, making my mother very tense. She would tell him off: *Why do you always have to clash things down?*

High up on the ladder, he had been struggling to fix an awkward piece of guttering. He had become annoyed and was grappling with it violently, his mind on the gutter and not on his safety. And then the ladder slipped.

Fortunately the hospital doctors were able to tell him that his spinal fracture would mend. A few weeks later he was sent home to lie on the dining room floor on his back for a further month or two. No doubt there were times when he feared that he might not walk or work again. We tip-toed around him while he lay there, but one day he suddenly spoke to me, possibly at my mother's bidding. This was one of the times when he was strangely formal, like when he had asked if I wanted to inherit the plumbing business. Now he said *I want to apologise for worrying you all.* He said that he had learned his lesson about losing his temper with his tools, and advised me to *never rush at things, it's not worth it.*

The main worry, of course, was money. My mother had always made something of an issue out of money, mainly because my father was barely making enough, and perhaps because she had all the responsibility for handling it. He came home with his pay packet at the end of every week, and handed it over to her. He then received his *baccy money*, and she put the rest somewhere safe to cover the expenses and bills for the coming week. At the same time she was quietly trying to save a little towards a rainy day, as well as towards a better future. She imagined that after her children had grown up, she would be able to afford a decent retirement in a nicer house. For now, though, money was always tight.

So with my father lying on the floor, there was great fear of financial disaster. I imagined that I would have to leave school early (the leaving age was 15 then), and my dreams would be over. My mother tried to say that things were not too bad at the moment, as my sister was now working and bringing a wage home. But I knew that I was guilty of being a drain on the family resources, and how would I be able to justify staying on at school in these circumstances?

However, there was no disaster. It was very fortunate that my father had left the family business, as grandad (the *ould devil*) would never have made enough provision for this kind of accident and sick leave. Being employed by Gateshead Council, he was now in a civilised sick pay scheme, and his job was kept open until he was fit enough to return. And indeed when he did return to work, he even had some extra money in the form of an industrial injury payment.

My mother went a bit quiet with her nagging during that time. After all the poor man was literally down on the floor, and did not need kicking. However, later on she delivered her verdict for my benefit: *What a fool your da is, nearly killing himself just to mend a gutter for the Council. That lot on the Council wouldn't be so soft. They would look out for themselves.*

She wasn't really criticising the Council. After all, they were helping us with sick pay and job security for my father. Rather, she was now blaming the accident on his willingness to help others while forgetting the possible risks to himself. Perhaps he was rushing to fix the gutter, eager to please the tenants of the house. Or perhaps the foreman had told him to hurry up and go to a more urgent job. Being in a rush had led to a loss of temper, which had led to a mistake. As far as my mother was concerned, it was a good example of why helping others should be avoided, as it will eventually land you in trouble.

Irritability *is a general mood in which there is reduced control over temper, usually resulting in verbal or behavioural outbursts, although the mood may also be present with no outwardly visible signs. It is subjectively unpleasant, and can be brief or prolonged. There is a distinction between anger as an emotion, which is a specific and shorter-lasting reaction to something, and an irritable mood, which is longer-lasting and generalises to things that might not normally make you angry (Snaith and Taylor 1985).*

Psychiatrists often see irritability as a minor part of a diagnosis such as anxiety or depression. However, it also exists in its own right. A person may bottle up anger about one specific thing, without resolving it, until the anger becomes a generalised mood. Or the mood may result from fatigue due to either overwork or insomnia (or withdrawal from an addictive drug).

Clearly a mood such as irritability would make my father more likely to get angry with an awkward task, and the distraction of that emotion would increase the chances of him making a mistake on the ladder. To that extent, my mother was correct to blame his temper for the accident. But what would have caused his irritability in the first place? Was it fatigue from overwork, or from snoring and poor sleep? Or could it have been the result of bottled-up feelings about her nagging?

Saying sorry *can be surprisingly helpful to all the parties involved. My father's apology was completely unexpected, but also touching. I had been feeling guilty for being a financial burden on him, while he was lying there on the floor incapacitated for all that time. How worried he must be, not knowing whether he would get back to work. Instead, he apologised for his fault in having the accident, said that he knew how we felt, and assured us that he would never let this happen again.*

You can't always apologise, of course. Life is tough and complicated, and you cannot smooth everything over. However, if you do decide to apologise, it is important to get it right. An incompetent apology is worse than none at all.

Identify what went wrong: you cannot apologise effectively if you are not clear what you are apologising for. Take full responsibility: even if other people contributed to the situation, you cannot apologise for them. Make no excuses: an apology with an excuse is not an apology. Choose the right time: usually the sooner the better, but sometimes the other person needs time to cool down before listening to you. Name the offence and admit that it affected the person: beware of weasel words which reduce your apology (for example: I am sorry if you were offended; I am sorry for any distress you might have felt). Don't go on about how bad you feel: it's not about you. Say how you can change yourself so that it won't happen again.

12

BUT I'M LIKE MY DA

1960

Maybe it is just traditional to say that a boy looks like his father. Certainly there was a degree of resemblance, probably more to do with our blue eyes and tallness than anything else. My mother and sister were brown-eyed and shorter. But does that mean that personality characteristics would also be inherited from the more similar parent? My mother clearly thought there was a danger of this, but maybe I could be saved if she kept on pointing out his faults.

Just once, my father was moved to tell me to *take no notice of your ma*. This was outside in the garden, beyond her hearing. He was unable to challenge her complaints about his appearance, his smoking and so on, but on one issue he believed he was on firmer ground. *Your ma seems to think you shouldn't help anyone*, he complained. He was angry after she had accused him of being soft for doing some kind of favour for a customer at work.

This was another lesson that she had tried to teach me: *You don't want to be bothering with folk.* She meant that other people were not to be trusted, or that they were a bad influence. If you were friendly and helpful to them, they would just take advantage. People were a bother, a nuisance, and life was much easier without them. In other words, my mother was *antagonistic* in personality, whereas my father was more *agreeable*. I could see his point of view on that. It was worrying to think that people might be as bad as my mother had painted them.

Another difference between my parents was that my father *knew how to do things*, whereas my mother had no great practical skills. This wasn't just a traditional gender difference, as she had no particular talent in the customary feminine skills such as sewing or cooking. Here again, my father sometimes got the blame. If she served up a poor meal, she would say that *he doesn't bring in enough money for anything better*.

He might have been lowly paid, but he had all sorts of practical abilities that we relied upon. His plumbing and other building trade skills were very useful at home whenever repairs were needed. If we had a burst pipe, which was a regular event in those freezing northern winters, there was no need to panic. Our plumber was on hand.

In the warmer weather there were his bee keeping skills, sorting through the internal workings of each hive, keeping them tidy and watching out for the queen bee. Unfortunately my mother's fear of being stung had rubbed off on me, and the best I could manage was to stand safely several feet away watching the bee-keeper at work.

And then there were his gardening skills, producing lots of vegetables. During the Second World War, everyone had been exhorted to *Dig for Victory*, and he had continued to do so. Potatoes were his speciality, and I enjoyed helping to dig the trenches to put them in, and then unearthing the splendid results later in the year.

In earlier years, when we were still in Consett, my father had also acquired enough skills as a motor mechanic to maintain his old plumber's van. Given the nature of vehicles in those days, it was important for a driver to know how to get going again after a breakdown. And my father's van had many such breakdowns. On weekend trips to the Durham moors, we often had picnics on the grass verge while he struggled with the engine or mended a puncture. However, after we moved to Gateshead the van was sold to a scrap dealer. It was no longer needed, as the Council plumbers were transported around their jobs by vans organised by the housing department. At other times, the Gateshead bus services were cheap and frequent, running everywhere that we needed to go. However, like my father, I preferred to walk wherever possible.

By the age of fifteen, I had been at Gateshead Grammar School for four years, and not a single practical skill had ever been mentioned. Physics and chemistry did involve some delicate manual adjustment of equipment, but subjects like woodwork, metalwork or gardening were only for less academic boys. This is a great shame, and later in life I discovered that many highly skilled craftsmen have high IQ's, which shouldn't really be a surprise when you remember that IQ covers visuospatial abilities as well as verbal ones. The issue of social class superiority really should not encourage you to restrict your range of skills.

If a grammar school boy was interested in practical skills, he would have to develop them at home. Like my father, I took up various hobbies, and particularly enjoyed making things. Early on I tried aircraft modelling, using balsa wood, paper and glue, but the planes tended to end in disappointment and a crash when actually launched into the air.

Then my father presented me with his crystal wireless set, which had been useful during the War because it did not require any sort of power supply. This was a device that you had to learn how to coax into action. You had to fiddle with the *cat's whisker*, which was a very fine wire which had to be touched with just the right amount of pressure against a lump of metallic crystalline material. This formed a primitive type of semi-conductor or diode. Getting it to work was a matter of trial and error until eventually the sound of a radio station (the Light Programme) emerged in your headphones. This was wonderfully magic.

In the following years, I acquired or built a series of more and more complicated short wave radios, spending many hours searching for obscure and distant stations. You could hear people and music from far-off lands all over the world. In my teenage years, this was as fascinating and addictive as the internet is today. Fortunately, I was able to retreat to my room to do all this, usually with headphones on.

My father's place of retreat was his shed, which was always dirty and untidy enough to repel most intruders. Here he tinkered with his bee equipment, but a lot of the time he simply sat and smoked, and then fell asleep. In the winter he sat by the warmth of the fire in the kitchen, sometimes falling asleep, but sometimes doing the crossword in the daily newspaper. He seldom managed to complete it, but seemed to enjoy the challenge of the puzzle.

Identification with parents has long been considered a normal part of childhood development, generating a variety of psychological theories ranging from Freud and other psychoanalysts to more modern Social Learning Theory (Bandura, Albert 1977). The simple fact is that a child is most attached to, and dependent upon, his parents (or whoever is mainly in charge of him), and therefore will be considerably (but not exclusively) influenced by them. He might consider them to be role models, to be generally followed in all ways. Or he might be selective in imitating specific aspects of them.

This process might not be all one way, of course. Parent and child could exert a mutual influence on each other, thus becoming even more similar in that respect. There could also be an appearance of influence where there is none. For example a child could develop a behaviour or style of behaviour which is inborn, but which resembles the parent's behaviour (this could be hereditary or just coincidence). It might then be encouraged to develop further because of the similarity with the parent.

In adolescence, of course, the child may be struggling to break free of some of these parental influences, but this is not easy. If he is successful, he might go too far and throw out the baby with the bathwater.

Agreeableness and Antagonism *are opposite ways of connecting with other people. Do you bring them closer to you, forming a bond, or do you keep them at arm's length? Do you help and trust them, or defend yourself by going on the attack?*

Being caring is by definition unselfish, but of course it can be rewarding for you as well. It makes you feel good, and others may admire you for it. However, if you are a habitually caring person, others might suspect you of being a do-gooder, naively blind to the parasitic nature of some people who beg for help. Occasionally there is much truth in this, and you should be careful about who you care for.

Agreeableness and antagonism form one of the factors or dimensions of human personality. Some extreme characters show fixed attitudes to other people, being either always agreeable or always antagonistic. However, most people manage to keep a balance, in which they are agreeable most of the time but can be antagonistic when it becomes necessary for self-defence.

Sadly, antagonism is often seen as more interesting than agreeableness (hence all the television and film entertainments involving hostilities). When my mother kept pointing out my father's faults, this probably captured my attention more than a list of his boring virtues. How would I manage to achieve a balance between all these things?

13

THE FIRST SYMPTOMS

1960

It all crept up on me very stealthily around the age of fifteen. If I had known how it would develop later, I would have been very frightened. But I knew nothing (and would not have believed it anyway).

It started in a small way, on the daily walk between school and home. Occasionally there were some actual hazards to contend with on the way home, but these were easy to tackle compared with the more nebulous worries that came later. For example, there was a secondary modern lad who started to make a habit of waiting for me and grabbing my satchel of books, in a joking sort of way but strangely saying nothing. While I was busy clutching my violin case he knew that I did not have enough hands to fend him off. His game was to run off with my satchel and then dump it further up the street. But one day I decided I had had enough, and I put down my violin and chased him. I was a fast runner and nearly caught him, much to his surprise. He never appeared on my way home again.

Then there was the thuggish lad who suddenly came up alongside me and punched me on the jaw, very hard, accusing me of looking *gormless*. At the time I was actually trying to develop a stoical attitude, carrying on walking and shouldering my books despite the fatigue of all those miles back and forth to school. So this was a good chance to demonstrate my grammar school stiff upper lip to this Neanderthal. For a second I felt the pain of his fist on my jaw, and even thought that I might fall over, but nothing happened and I carried on walking without a pause, as if I had scarcely noticed. A woman who had seen the hardness of the blow stopped me to ask if I was all right. *Fine*, I said, as you do. And indeed it was true enough, the pain having eased by the time I got home. I never saw that lad again, either.

These were the only actual examples of bullying that I ever experienced, but I did sense a sort of threat on the streets whenever I was in my grammar school uniform. By keeping my head down and using the quiet side streets, I was able to minimise this. It wasn't difficult to work out that all this jealousy and aggression was not really my war. I was being caught in the cross-fire of a class war in which I did not belong to either side. One of these days, when I became an adult, I would be able to leave all this behind. In earlier childhood I had sometimes dreaded growing up, but now I longed for adulthood as if it would be the answer to all my problems.

After keeping my head down metaphorically, I started to do it literally. Having grown to six feet tall by the age of 15, I felt very conspicuous, especially as I had not grown any wider and looked very skinny. One day when walking through the crowds in Northumberland Street, the main shopping area in Newcastle, I noticed that I could see above the heads of all the shoppers. That felt weird. Although I was glad to be tall, because it looked grown up, I hated to stand out from the crowd. In this respect, I had become a normally self-conscious teenager. Having grown faster than many of my classmates, I was subjected to the usual jokes such as *what's the weather like up there?* So I tried to hide my height by walking with my head down, but of course this only made me even more conspicuous.

Then my eyes started to water as I walked along the street. There was probably a good reason for this, namely the bitingly icy wind blowing into my face during the worst of the winter in the North-East. Sheriff Hill is the highest spot in Gateshead, at 500 feet above sea level, and from the top of a double decker bus on a clear day you can glimpse the North Sea and the Durham coast about ten miles away. It can be a very draughty place, and indeed I once saw a corrugated metal roof being blown off a garage by that wind.

My eyes must have become sensitised after repeated exposure to the cold, and then they started watering even with a slight breeze. This led to me walking along holding my head down further, all tensed up against the wind. My eyes watered until I could hardly see where I was going. If anyone was about, I felt embarrassed in case they thought I was crying, so I always turned my head away to hide my eyes.

This eye-watering worried me for several months. Instead of realising that it was a normal reaction to the weather, I thought it was some kind of weakness of character. I hated the feeling that it was yet another cross for me to bear, like my height. Strangely, I wished that I could be old, so that I would need glasses and these would shield me against the wind. I should have wrapped myself up more, or I could have gone on the bus rather than struggling to walk. But I was stubbornly stoical and just carried on, wishing it would go away. And of course when the weather got warmer, my eyes did go back to normal.

But then the sun also could be a problem. Admittedly, we never seemed to see much of the sun in the North-East, especially with the fogs and smog around the industrial areas. Any sunshine was usually short-lasting, so people dressed for the rain and cold even in the summer. On the beach, men would wear their suits and ties, exposing their shirts only if the sun became particularly hot. My dad was always stoical in these circumstances, and had to be nagged by my mother: *For goodness sake take your jacket off, man, you look roasted!*

For me, the sun only seemed to appear at inconvenient moments. Climbing up the hill coming home from school, dressed for winter, with a satchel loaded with books on my back and a violin case in my hand, the clouds would suddenly clear away. By the time I reached home, I would be roasted, red and soaked with sweat. *Gritting my teeth and carrying on,* but feeling a fool.

But why, even when I had the opportunity to make myself more comfortable, was I too proud to do so? At the grammar school there was one particular classroom where the sun shone through the big windows at certain times of year, casting its light and heat on the spot where I normally sat. It was like having a gigantic heat lamp cooking my face. My eyes were dazzled, so I had to shield them with my hand in order to see the blackboard. There were plenty of other desks available, but this was my place and stubbornly I had to suffer it. As before, I was putting it all down to a weakness of my character, rather than a normal effect of sunshine. One afternoon the teacher noticed my plight and asked if I wanted to move to another desk in the shade. Unbelievably, I said *No, I'm all right,* and carried on roasting.

I had got into a vicious circle of self-consciousness, in which I tried to make myself inconspicuous by valiantly pretending that nothing was happening, but in fact this just drew more attention to me. My only strategy for coping was to *grit my teeth and carry on.* A teacher once announced to our class, for no apparent reason, that self-consciousness was absolutely normal in our teenage years, but it would simply go away as we got older. It was a thought that I often clung on to, longing to get to that magic age of adulthood. In the meantime I would just have to put up with these moments of teenage agony.

Cumulative stress *is produced when a person experiences one stressful situation after another, in such a way that all the stress adds up or accumulates over time. This would occur when the person is unable to resolve one problem before the next one starts. This could be because each stressful situation is severe and long-lasting, or alternatively there might be a lot of them (even if not severe) coming along frequently.*

The fact that stress can accumulate in this way creates various possible psychological traps for an unwary or inexperienced person. For example, it means that stressors do not have to be large and impressive. If there are enough small stressors, these can add up to a significant physical and mental effect. Secondly, there is a tipping point which occurs unexpectedly after sufficient stress has accumulated (the straw that breaks the camel's back). And finally there is the fact that the effects of cumulative stress can show up after an unexpectedly long time, such as from childhood into adulthood (Forehand et al 1998).

Although children and adolescents might (on average) have fewer stressors than adults (because they have no adult responsibilities such as work, relationships, family and children), they may be more vulnerable to any that they do have. Their lack of experience and wisdom will add to their difficulties (this applies to inexperienced adults as well, of course). Adolescents may also have problems peculiar to their stage of physical and mental development, even though they might appear to be nearly adult. For example, there is a certain part of the brain which is one of the last to develop before adulthood, and research suggests that it has something to do with self-consciousness. So perhaps it is true that this problem is part of teenage development, and of course it will add to the stress of anything else that is going on.

There was a significant danger in my stoical strategy for trying to cope with stress. I had learned from my academic studies that persistent hard work paid off by producing good marks. Applying the same strategy in dealing with stress can be successful in some circumstances, but not if you take it too far. In a situation where stress is accumulating from one day to the next, it would be better to try to avoid any further unnecessary stressful experiences. If you keep plodding on regardless, you are just storing up trouble.

The symptoms of stress *are generally worth noting as dispassionately as possible. It is common either to persist in fruitless worrying about symptoms, or alternatively paying no heed, but neither of these single strategies does any good. One of the classic processes in the development of stress disorders is the Vicious Circle, in which stress first generates physical symptoms, and then you worry about them (for example: my heart is thumping, maybe there is something wrong with it?) But this worry in turn generates more stress and more symptoms, and so it goes on. In my case, I first tried to ignore the symptoms, and did not ask what was causing them, but this meant that I did not look at what I could do to change things.*

It is worth knowing that stress can cause the following kinds of symptoms, and that they are telling you to look at yourself and your life to see what might be producing them. The answer to that question may not be obvious. Or actually it might be perfectly obvious, but you are failing to see it.

Anxiety *(an urge to avoid or escape from danger) includes:*
    Thumping heart, fast pulse.
    Shaking, especially your hands (for example when holding a cup or a pen).
    Over-active bowel or bladder.
    Hot and sweaty, red in the face.
    Breathing too fast and too shallow, feeling short of breath.

Tension *(muscles held in readiness for action) includes:*
  Restlessness, fidgeting.
  Aches and pains, especially in your shoulders and neck.
  Headaches.
  Indigestion, especially from eating too quickly.
  Difficulty getting to sleep.

Fatigue *(the effect of having done too much) includes:*
  Tired all the time, not helped by sleep.
  Poor concentration and memory.
  Feeling faint, weak or giddy.

Anger *(ready to fight, either physically or verbally) includes:*
  Temper, shouting at or hitting someone or something.
  Violent thoughts about taking revenge.
  Self-harm, cutting yourself or attempting suicide.

Depression *(over-awareness of the harsh realities of human existence)*
includes:
  Sadness and weeping, grief over a loss.
  Guilt, repeatedly wondering if something was your fault.
  Suicidal thoughts, wishing you were dead.
  Loss of appetite, not eating.

14

STARS OVER WREKENTON

1960

My mother was on the move again. There was no garden at our house in Egremont Drive, just a back yard with a shed, so we had acquired an allotment some distance away. It was difficult to carry gardening things to and fro, especially now that my father had acquired a bad back. A house with a big garden would be much easier. As well as this, my mother was fed up with the Sheriff Hill area, which had a rather poor choice of shops. And probably she was simply bored, with no interests beyond the house. She had no friends, and there was very little contact with neighbours. A new house would reinvigorate her.

We moved to Long Bank in Wrekenton, an area on the southern outskirts of Gateshead. The County Durham countryside could be glimpsed to the south and west, and there was a Co-operative Society food store just up the road. My mother was always comfortable with the Co-op. On the other side of the road from our house there were green fields, illuminated sometimes by the glow of a setting sun. A previous owner had given the house an apt name: *Sunlea*.

In time, of course, these green fields would be covered in concrete and tarmac, with ever increasing housing estates, and my mother would feel the need to move on again. And even further in the future, the Angel of the North would stand just half a mile or so down the hill on the main route to Newcastle.

But in 1960 the view from the front of the house was pleasantly green. To the back of the house was a long and useful garden, with space for vegetables and bee hives. And there was an old air raid shelter left over from the War, half submerged under a weedy earth bank.

The only snag was that there were only two bedrooms, so my father had to start building a partition wall, made of rather flimsy hardboard, down the centre of the main bedroom. I would sleep on one side of this, while my parents slept on the other. My sister had the small bedroom at the back of the house. My mother was hoping that this partition would be only a temporary measure, as my sister was now 21 and could be expected to fly the nest. On the southern side of the hardboard my room was quite small, but big enough for a narrow bed, an alcove with hanging rail for clothes, and a small table where I could do my homework. Soon it would also become a workshop for the making of a telescope.

Having become interested in astronomy, I had played with a small hand-held telescope but its limitations were soon apparent. What I needed was something much more impressive, such as a six-inch reflector telescope with a proper mount. There was no way of affording to buy such a thing, but maybe I could make one. A book from the library had given me this idea. I was very familiar with Gateshead Public Library, which was only a short walk from the Grammar School. In fact I had borrowed at least two books per week since the age of eleven, and had worked my way through most of the novels, so I was now exploring the non-fiction. There was a book which explained in great detail, and very clearly, how to make a telescope (Howard 1959). I borrowed this repeatedly for the next six months.

It is hard to recall, let alone believe, how I managed to achieve this at the age of fifteen. However, the book explains the various techniques very clearly, and you just follow the instructions. You buy two six-inch diameter discs of inch thick glass, and patiently grind one against the other, using carborundum powder to wear away the surface so that one disc becomes concave, while the other becomes convex. The concave one will become the mirror. Gradually, using finer and finer carborundum powder, and eventually jeweller's rouge, you produce a perfect parabolic concave glass. All along the way, of course, you are testing and measuring it to achieve the correct shape and quality. This included setting up an optical test with a sodium lamp, involving lying on the floor of the upstairs landing in the dark, peering at the reflection from the soon-to-be mirror. After much checking and re-checking for a perfect result, I took the glass to be silvered, turning it into the finished parabolic telescope mirror. After some woodwork to construct a frame, with a prism and eyepiece to magnify the image, I now had a telescope. In the middle of the back garden, I constructed a mount for it out of heavy plumbing parts and concrete, and placed a wooden cover around it with a removable roof.

It was now ready for action, and with great excitement I waited for a clear starlit night. The view through the telescope was amazing. The moon was magnified hugely, and only a small part of it could be seen in the eyepiece. You could imagine yourself coming in to land on one of these astounding craters. And as for the stars, there were just so many of them, thousands and thousands that you cannot see with the naked eye. Although I did try to identify stars and nebulae by using a star chart, it was also wonderful just pointing the telescope anywhere in the sky. The beauty of the stars was thrilling. And one night there was something that did not need the telescope. The sky was covered in greenish waves of light, and it took a moment before I realised that this was the Northern Lights (the aurora borealis). This was something I had never seen before, and after summoning my parents to have a look, it seemed that they had never seen it either. Even the north-east of England is not usually northerly enough. It was very lucky that I happened to be outside and looking upwards at the time.

But all this excitement was soon to crash down, literally. The winds in this part of the world were regularly vicious, and one morning I got up to discover that the shelter I had built around the telescope had flown away, smashing everything in its path. Poking around in the wreckage, I found my precious mirror broken in two. My heart too was broken, and I felt numb, not to mention stupid. Why had I not brought my telescope back into the safety of the house?

But strangely my grief did not last for very long. The existence of the telescope seemed to matter less than the fact that I had achieved the making of it. Yes, I had been thrilled to see the amazing images that it produced, but that was as far as it went. I wasn't sure that I really wanted to spend hours in the freezing cold darkness trying to do serious observations. So maybe it was all for the best. I could still boast that I had made my own telescope.

Conscientiousness *is one of the Five Factors of personality (McCrae and Costa 2003). It is the trait of being painstaking and careful, or the quality of acting according to the principles of conscience. It includes elements such as self-discipline, carefulness, thoroughness, organization, deliberation, and need for achievement. Conscientious individuals are generally hard working and reliable. If taken to the extreme, however, they may also be workaholics, perfectionists, or obsessive-compulsives.*

I had learned to enjoy the process of achieving things through careful and prolonged hard work. However, the actual product was relatively immaterial. This can be a great mistake, as it leads to work for work's sake. If work has no result, it is simply a waste of energy, a self-inflicted cause of stress and fatigue.

At least, that is the scientific way of looking at these things. I don't want any remarks about broken mirrors and seven years bad luck.

Worrying *can actually be a very sensible thing to do. It involves thinking ahead and being on the alert for possible dangers or misfortunes, in order to avoid, prevent or minimise them. However, it is not purely cold rational thinking. There is an instinctive emotional component, a degree of anxiety, which alerts you to do something about the possible danger. For some reason I did not worry about the possibility of my telescope getting blown away. Perhaps by then I was too tired after all the effort of constructing it.*

I was well aware of the strength of the local winds, and well aware of the fragility of glass. 'What if?' would have been a good question. A risk assessment would have looked at the combination of Dangerousness and Likelihood. If something would be dangerous but its occurrence is highly unlikely, it is not worth spending much time on. On the other hand, something that is moderately likely is indeed worth thinking about, even if it is only moderately dangerous. I should have had the foresight to worry about the safety of my mirror. That would have led me to take precautions, such as strengthening its shelter, or simply taking it inside when not in use.

Having a worry, finding a possible answer, and then putting the problem to one side, is much more useful than not having the worry in the first place. There are many risky events and situations in life, and quite often they take us by surprise because, strangely, we assume that these things only happen to other people. Sometimes we should be more aware of common dangers, such as accidents on the roads or elsewhere. Many accidents are caused by not concentrating on the task in hand, and by not allowing enough time or space to respond to the unexpected.

15

ON THE BUSES

1961

After our move to Wrekenton, it had become a little too far to walk to school. One mile from Sheriff Hill was reasonable, but a three mile trek from Wrekenton was impractical, especially now with an even bigger load of books in my satchel for GCE O-level homework. So I started to use the buses, which were always reliable, frequent and cheap, but very crowded at school times.

These were the old style double-deckers, with the open platform at the rear where you climbed on and jumped off. I enjoyed riding on the upper deck, where you could see the passing view and look down on people. But so did everyone else, especially all the other schoolchildren going home. They liked to be upstairs, out of the view of the conductor, so that they could mess about and make a noise. The upper deck was always full by the time I got on the bus, later on the route.

If the lower deck was also crowded, you just had to stand, and this I did not mind at all, hanging on the rail attached above our heads. But all too often I was cursed by having to sit in the one seat that I really hated. It was always the only seat left (was that because no one else would sit there?), and the conductor would point me in its direction. He would not let me stand if there was a seat still available. This dreaded seat was the one just behind the driver. It faced forward, looking at the opaque glass screen at the back of the driver's seat. And reflected in that glass you could see yourself. Your face was right there, in front of you, in your face. And just to make it even worse, the whole bus load of people could be seen behind you, with all of their eyes looking forward and meeting yours in the glass.

As I sat there, in a misery of self-consciousness, the sun would come out, shining through the side window and illuminating my reflection in the glass. I would feel myself go hot and red and sweaty. Trying not to look at myself in the glass, my eyes caught the eyes of the passengers behind me. So I lowered my head to study the floor, but as soon as I looked up I could see all these eyes again. The journey was only fifteen minutes long, but it seemed interminable, especially on the long stretch up the steep hill where the fully laden bus laboured rather slowly. I could feel my whole body trickling and steaming with sweat. When I reached my stop and could rush away from the bus, the relief was like the cessation of an agonising pain.

This happened again and again, several times a week, getting worse and worse. I could think of no solution. It was now happening even when I managed to get a seat elsewhere on the bus. I tried to delay my journey by going to the library for an hour after school, but then discovered that the buses were still crowded until quite late. So I just had to *grit my teeth and carry on*, in the hope that it would all just wear off when I got older. That's what that teacher had said. And after all, it was only for half an hour every day.

But it started to spread. Every day some situation would arise where I became hot and self-conscious. I became anxious in advance, knowing what would happen. This was fear of the fear. My stomach cringed and my heart thumped fast and loud. I felt more and more that my shame was visible to any passing stranger. I was going red in the face: *look at the state of that*, they were thinking. I was sweating from all parts of the body: *he smells of sweat,* they thought. My heart was pounding: *there's something wrong with him,* they would think. I was totally embarrassed: *What a fool,* they seemed to say.

Passing strangers seemed to be focussing upon me with all their senses. I could almost hear what they were thinking, and they were looking at me with derision. Trying to ignore them, I *gritted my teeth and carried on.* As soon as I got back home and went to my room, I calmed down and tried to forget it. And at my desk at school, I was all right. These were safe places.

Then it spread even further, to meal times. To eat with someone else is to invite them to watch you doing awkward and undignified acts, namely the process of getting food into your mouth, and then the chewing and swallowing of it. Most people think nothing of this, but if you are self-conscious you will know the horror of feeling how it must look. And the question of what people must be thinking when they see you going hot and sweaty over your food.

Fortunately, my teenage lifestyle involved very little eating out, except for the occasional fish and chips in a seaside café with my parents. There wasn't a great deal of dining out for most people in the North-East in those days. My difficulty actually started at home, which was strange as I ate most of my meals there on my own. Indeed the whole family tended to eat separately, each one coming home at a different time and being served immediately by mother. She too ate separately, liking to have her own meal earlier, or eating at the little table in the kitchen while serving my meal in the dining room. I was in the habit of reading the daily newspaper next to my plate on the table, eating quietly on my own.

But then the simple act of eating started to make me feel hot and sweaty, at which point I would dread anyone coming in and seeing me. Hot food and drinks were the worst, but just the act of chewing seemed to generate heat in my face. On the odd occasion when I sat at the table with my sister or mother, I began to feel self-conscious about feeling hot. This anxiety would then generate further heat, and my heart would thump. I became a rather fast eater, so that I could finish and retreat upstairs to my room to cool down. This cooling-off time gradually worsened from ten minutes to a whole hour.

But never mind, I was still all right at other times. School lessons were fine, and that was the most important thing at the moment. I could just *grit my teeth and carry on*. One day I will get older and it will go away.

Social phobia (or social anxiety disorder) *means that an intense fear is habitually triggered in a person by certain social situations, or more generally by any situation involving other people (Butler 2008). It causes considerable distress and impaired ability to function in at least some parts of everyday life. Physical symptoms of this fear include excessive blushing, sweating, trembling, palpitations, nausea, and stammering or rapid speech. Panic attacks may develop. Anyone who suffers from this will suffer alone, as it is particularly hard for them to seek help.*

The person is anxious about characteristics of themselves that he perceives to be deficient, and which may be exposed to critical public scrutiny. For example, he feels that he has inferior social skills (such as being unable to think of anything to say, or not knowing the right etiquette). Or he feels that he is no good at concealing any symptoms of anxiety (such as blushing or shakiness in his hands). Or perhaps he has the idea that there are significant flaws in his physical appearance (for example hair a mess, or nose the wrong shape, or too fat or too thin). Overall, the person may regard themselves as having an inadequate personality of some kind, such as being boring, stupid, ignorant, or miserable.

Social phobia typically starts in early adolescence, and onset after the age of 25 is rare. It often occurs alongside low self-esteem and clinical depression, due to lack of personal relationships and long periods of isolation. To try to reduce their anxiety and alleviate depression, older teenagers and young adults with social phobia may unwisely use alcohol or other drugs, leading to problems with these as well.

After starting in a minor way, social anxiety tends to develop in the same way that all other phobias do, building upon themselves. Each experience of anxiety lays a foundation for further anxiety on the next occasion, because you start to build up some anxiety in anticipation of the situation. Then if you cannot find any way of controlling the anxiety, apart from escaping from the situation, you will be even more anxious about what will happen the next time. Purely gritting your teeth and carrying on, without adding a smarter strategy, will just make things worse.

But how would I know that? I was an ignorant inexperienced teenager, and not likely to ask anyone's advice. And would anyone have known what to do? Very unlikely, I think.

Keep calm and carry on *is fine if you can actually keep calm. Unfortunately, I had reached the stage of making a drama out of my stress symptoms, thus causing them to grow. By imagining that the entire world could see what I was feeling, my anxiety was increased tenfold. Most of the time, these feelings are nothing more than the ordinary emotions of everyday life, but they do carry an instinctive alarm function. There is just a possibility that they are a warning signal, so then your imagination will start wondering what is wrong. But you will worry about the wrong things. For example:*

A fast or thumping heart *is a common symptom of stress, sometimes leading you to worry about what might be wrong with your heart. On the contrary your health may be benefiting from this exercise to the heart. You would be wise to ignore these fears about illness, and instead focus on identifying the real stress in your life.*

Tremor or shaking *shows mostly in the hands, but can be elsewhere in the body. If people are watching while you are signing your name, or holding a cup, or using tools, your self-consciousness will make you shake even more. You might fear that you are losing control of yourself, but this not the case. Ignore that idea, and try to work out what is really happening in your life to cause this.*

Going hot and sweating *is another example of the excess physical energy produced by anxiety. If you had just run a mile, you would think nothing of the fact that you are wet with sweat and have gone red in the face. But because you are feeling anxious, you imagine that you are now a conspicuous beacon of social failure. And that you are attracting the attention of any passing stranger. Ignore that idea, and look for the real reason for having become so anxious.*

Aches and pains *result from muscles being tensed up through stress, as much as through physical strain. The head, neck and shoulders are the usual places. The drama begins when you get the idea that there might be something physically wrong, such as cancer or a brain tumour. People often worry about such things even when a doctor has ruled them out. Ignore that worry, and try to identify the actual stress in your life.*

Exhaustion *seems quite normal if you have been working excessively or sleeping poorly. But if you haven't, your imagination will come up with some dramatic illness from which you might die. However, don't forget that powerful emotions such as anxiety, anger or depression can be very wearing, and can build up over a long time. That kind of fatigue can be difficult to shake off even if you have managed a short period of rest. Ignore your sense of impending doom, and just give yourself time to recover.*

Poor concentration and memory *can be the result of stress, fatigue and depression. However, a common worry is that there is something wrong with your brain. This is actually fairly unlikely, but if you are seriously worried, your doctor could arrange some* *tests to make sure. You could of course try to reassure yourself with the fact that an imperfect memory is absolutely normal. Ignore your worry, and try to improve your memory by making sure that you are paying proper attention to things in the first place (or make notes!). Fortunately, at this stage my youthfulness was helping to protect my memory and concentration. But eventually these too would suffer.*

16

TAKING THE PRIZE

1961

Despite all my problems, I was still doing well at school. I was coming up to 16 years old, and this was the year when we would take our GCE O-level exams. Some pupils had left when they were 15, as the law allowed, but what was the point of going to grammar school and then not taking these exams?

At the age of 13 we had been asked to select our subjects for the GCE. In my case I gladly dropped Latin, Religious Education, Music and Art, to give more time for my preferred subjects: Mathematics, Physics, Chemistry, English Language, English Literature, French, History and Geology. *You can take more exams than this, but we think that eight is enough for anybody,* we were told by the teacher. I was happy with that.

It was made less stressful by taking three of the exams in the winter, and the remaining five in the summer. It was also made easier by the fact that we were 16 years old, an age at which people are approaching their peak of memory ability (declining again from their 20's onwards!). *If you cannot think how to answer the question, just quote the poem or book from memory,* advised the English Literature teacher. *That usually impresses them.*

I scored six A grades and two B's. These marks were the highest in the school for that year, and there was a prize for this, which was unexpected. The prize was most impressive, being the magnificent sum of fifty pounds. Bearing in mind that the average weekly wage at that time was a bit less than twenty pounds, and ten years previously my father had earned only five pounds per week, my mother was quite incredulous. *Are you sure they haven't made a mistake?*

I gave the money to my mother *to help towards my upkeep, now that I'm staying on at school.* This was still giving me a lot of guilt. My mother had always complained about never having enough money, blaming my father for this. In fact the bills were always paid and we were never really short of our basic needs, but I remained under the impression that the family was always on a financial knife-edge. My mother would not be able to sleep easy until her children were in good jobs and paying their way. My sister was already bringing money home, which left me as the main burden.

Although my mother had always encouraged me to do well at school, the idea of staying on after the age of 16 was something completely beyond her experience. I had not told her that it might even lead to university, and therefore I would not get a job until I was in my twenties. That would have been like telling her that I was going to the moon. Why should I waste more years at school when I could show my exam results now and get a nice job in an office? In no time I would be earning more than my father, and paying my way at home.

But I had already told the school that I would be staying on to do A-levels, so now I tried to explain to my mother that this would lead to a job considerably better than anything she had ever imagined (*but surely there aren't any jobs in mathematics round here,* she scoffed). In fact I had no idea what it would lead to, but my classmates were staying on, and they seemed to think that it was a perfectly normal thing to do.

I explained to no one that I was in a mess of anxiety, of the sort that could easily blight these plans. In fact, the whole idea of leaving school and moving on, whether to a job or to university, made me sick with dread. How could I face new people and new situations, when I was being reduced to a sweating wreck just sitting on a bus? But maybe if I stayed on in the Sixth Form it would give me a bit more time to reach that magical age when I was supposed to grow out of my anxiety.

Not that I called it *anxiety* at that time. My only diagnostic concepts were *self-consciousness* and *suffering from your nerves*. These were things that were best kept quiet. I had never heard anyone, either at school or within my family, talking about them. If someone did mention such phrases, it was only a passing mention before a swift change of subject.

My education continued to have less and less relevance to these important personal matters. Now in the Sixth Form, my specialised school subjects were focussed on the pursuit of three A-level exams. I had chosen to do Pure Maths, Applied Maths and Physics, a rather elite combination according to one of the teachers. However, as far as I was concerned mathematics was simply convenient, as it depended upon doing lots of private study on my own. It did not require group activities, outings or expensive books or materials.

There were only four of us in this class, with an excellent maths teacher called Louis Theakstone, who relieved our mutual boredom from time to time by telling us something about himself. Having been brought up in Russia before the Second World War, he spoke fluent Russian and had worked as an interpreter during the War. He showed us a photograph of himself at the Yalta conference, with people such as Churchill, Roosevelt and Stalin. We were very impressed at this, especially the idea that a teacher could have had a life other than in school.

Would we like to learn a bit of Russian, he asked, and somewhat warily we expressed an interest. Russian was becoming a very fashionable language, and not just because of the Cold War. There was a lot of science developing in the Soviet Union, and it would be useful if some of our scientists could read their publications. So we started with the alphabet and its exotic sounds, which were even more extraordinary than our Geordie accent. The strange symbols set us quite a challenge, a bit like using a mathematical code.

School was beginning to feel quite adult now. Sometimes it seemed as if the real prize was in sight, namely growing up into a world where I would have a really interesting and well-paid job. And where I would have the confidence to do whatever I wanted. But in fact I was spending more and more time at home. In the Sixth Form, we were allowed to go home to do private study if there were no lessons, and this enabled me to go early and avoid the rush hour on the buses. Twice a week it was a great relief not to have that anxiety, but then I started to feel uneasy about having all this time on my own. It made going out seem even harder.

Social class mobility *in Britain is (on average) significantly related to intelligence. Although there may be individual exceptions, and many other factors will have an influence, intelligence still has the single strongest effect (Nettle 2003). Scores on an intelligence test at age 11 are a significant predictor (all other things being equal) of people's occupational class in middle age, whatever class their parents belonged to. However, for any individual person, other factors may have an even greater influence: personality, values, health, and life events.*

In my case, I had long since left my parents miles behind in terms of education, and was being pushed onwards by the school and by my ambitious intellectual interests. At the same time I was being pushed in the opposite direction by two very strong psychological forces. There is a loyalty, or at least an attachment, to your original parental class, or to your other roots (in my case being a Geordie, for example). I could not imagine being a professional person (which might even involve becoming some sort of Southerner), if only because I had no idea how such people lived. This fear of the unknown was then multiplied in my case by a continually developing social phobia. If I went to University, I would have to leave home and this would mean no hiding place. I would have to eat in public dining rooms, for example. How could I do that?

I was faced with many impending changes, with no knowledge of how to deal with them. But it wasn't a lack of desire to explore new horizons. After all, I wanted to be a scientist and make new discoveries. It was just that I had no idea how to reach that goal, and no one that I could really ask. My mother had long ago said that my education had taken me beyond anything that she or my father could understand, and that I would have to ask the school if I needed to know anything. But at the school I did not know what I needed to ask, or whether anyone would have an answer.

How would I be able to join the educated and professional social class, when I was clearly just a Geordie lad? How would I be able to leave home and move to some university town, when neither I nor my parents had ever been further south than Scarborough or Blackpool, and mostly no further than Whitley Bay? These were very daunting prospects, even without my developing state of phobic anxiety. It would have been easier to settle down where I was, and to keep to what I knew. Except of course that this was no longer possible.

Talk to someone: *this is what I should have done at this stage, before things got any more difficult. However, there is a stigma attached to mental health problems (there shouldn't be, but there is), making people reluctant to talk about them. In fact all sorts of personal matters may be hard to get off your chest. Even when other people actually have no problem with your problem, you still fear their reaction. But bottling up your worries will only make them grow bigger, so it is* worth trying to find someone to tell. Choose your listener carefully, of course. It is surprising how many people cannot listen for long without interrupting or criticising.

If your problems are making you unwell (mental illness can feel as bad as any physical disorder), your doctor might be the obvious person to tell. This can also be a route to a counsellor, psychologist or psychiatrist, as your general practitioner can refer you. A psychiatrist, by the way, is a specialist mental health doctor with a prescription pad and hospital beds, who will also do some talking therapy. Psychologists and counsellors are non-medical and mainly do talking therapies or re-training programmes.

Having said all that, it is not always easy, even in the present day, to find the right person to talk to. If at first you don't succeed, try someone else.

17

CRASHING OUT

1962

Coming up to the age of seventeen, there was one particular day at school when my mind went missing. For the first time in my life I could not understand what the teacher was writing on the blackboard. And more than that, *I couldn't be bothered to try*. This was a shocking experience. It was the death of my only remaining hope. What was the point of enduring all that horrible anxiety if I wasn't achieving anything at school? *Face reality*, I told myself, *I might as well give up*. Forget all these silly dreams about becoming a mathematician, or even an astronomer. How could a lad from Gateshead do anything like that, anyway?

I feel sick, I told my mother, not entirely untruthfully, to explain why I was staying at home the next morning. By the afternoon, I had made up my mind. *I'm going to leave school and get a job*. My mother hesitated for a second, but then looked quite cheerful. *Well, if you're sure*, she said. She had suspected for a long time that I was fooling myself with all this high-flown nonsense spouted by school teachers who have no idea what real life is like.

A few days later, the school's reaction was to write and ask for their £50 prize back. *Just tell them we've spent it*, advised my mother as I set off to see the headmaster. The prize was for pupils who stayed on at school, he claimed. This was a surprise to me. No one had said that there were any conditions beyond having achieved the highest marks. When I was given the prize, I was not only proud of myself, I felt really grateful to the school. But now this all collapsed. *Bugger off*, I thought to myself (although this was not the sort of language that I had ever used out loud). My gratitude disappeared, and I was suddenly feeling angry at this man who seemed interested only in his prize. I had made myself ill, working to achieve those grades, but he had no idea about that and I did not enlighten him. *We can't afford to give it back. My father is on a low income.* I waved my social class at him and felt proud for once. *I'm not well,* I explained as my reason for leaving. He seemed unconvinced, but enquired no further. He let me go.

I applied for a job as a junior audit clerk in an accountants' office in Newcastle. My ability to do mental arithmetic got me through the interview with ease, and I was appointed on a trial basis. The pay was only two pounds and ten shillings per week, but there were said to be better prospects eventually if I studied for the professional qualifications.

The accountants' office was quiet, with quiet people who made me feel fairly comfortable. My problem of eating in front of other people was not too bad, as we all brought sandwiches and ate them in our own little corner. But the work was mind-numbingly boring, and I lasted only a few weeks. The only interesting event was a trip out with one of the accountants to a shipyard on the Tyne, with the depressing conclusion that *some of these shipyards are going to go bust one of these days* (he was quite right).

My job was to check through small business accounts, adding up thousands of small sums in my head. This was long before businesses had electronic tills and accountants had easy calculators or computers. The end came for me one day when I was checking a shopkeeper's account book which contained hundreds of errors. As soon as I had corrected a column, another big bunch of errors in the next column would upset it again. One of the accountants tried to reassure me that I wasn't losing my mind: *These shopkeepers cannot add up. Don't worry about getting it perfect, 95 per cent accuracy is good enough.* But a sense of utter futility overcame me.

I feel sick, I said to my mother again. *I don't think I can carry on with this job.* Her heart must have sunk at this news. *Have a few days off, and then see,* she advised. But things looked no different after a few days, so that was the end of that. I declared that I was unwell, but did not specify my sickness. *Don't know,* I said, like a stereotypical teenager. Inside I knew that I was guilty of being a total burden on my family, and there was now no prospect of ever being anything else. *Go to bed and rest,* instructed my mother. This was her infallible strategy for dealing with sickly children and husbands. If they were genuinely ill, then a rest would be the cure. But if they were malingering, they would soon get bored in bed and would declare themselves better.

So I went to my room and rested. I had no intention of declaring myself better. In fact I hoped that this would be my death bed. Perhaps I had some wonderfully serious illness that would finish me off. That would be a good way of getting rid of all these problems.

Clinical Depression significantly affects a person's family and personal relationships, as well as their work or school life. There is usually a very low mood, pervading all aspects of life, and an inability to experience pleasure in activities that were formerly enjoyed. Depressed people may be preoccupied with thoughts and feelings of worthlessness, inappropriate guilt or regret, helplessness, hopelessness, and self-hatred. Other symptoms include poor concentration and memory, withdrawal from social situations and activities, reduced sex drive, and thoughts of death or suicide. Insomnia is common, and typically the person wakes in the early hours (e.g. 4 am) and cannot get back to sleep. Appetite often decreases, with resulting weight loss.

It is common for depression in adolescents to have been preceded by anxiety, but not the other way around (Cole et al 1998). Clinicians would be wise to provide early intervention or depression prevention counselling to children or adolescents who present with signs of anxiety.

Gratitude *and* **Guilt** *can become a problem for conscientious people, who may have great difficulty in accepting help from others or being dependent on them. They feel guilty about owing anything to anyone, and may be so concerned to do something in return, that they forget to express any words of gratitude for the original favour. But a simple thank you is all that is required, and this may be appreciated as much as the repayment of the debt.*

A child's first experience of debt is his dependency on his parents. Hopefully, all that they want in return is that he should look reasonably grateful (teenagers can be disappointing in this regard, of course). It is a tricky balance, but certainly children should not feel guilty for being a financial burden. My mother always made me painfully aware that we were short of money, and that this would change only when I grew up and got a job. She was presumably just expressing her own anxieties about money, and I absorbed these into myself.

Winning the school prize and giving her the money helped to relieve a little bit of that guilt, and I felt very grateful to the school for awarding it to me. But when the headmaster wanted to take it back, my gratitude ceased and was replaced by anger. This enabled me to hang on to my prize without any guilt whatsoever, feeling perfectly entitled to it. I had earned it, and my mother needed it.

But then I started to feel vaguely angry with my mother, too, perhaps triggered by my experience with the headmaster. These people,

I thought, have no idea of what I am going through. Indeed, they show no interest, ask no questions, and make no comment. There is no sign that I could ask them for help, or that they would know how to help. So why should I feel guilty about not doing what they want?

18

RETREAT

1963

At the age of 17 – 18, I stayed in my room for nearly a year, which in hindsight seems an astonishing amount of time. My memories of this phase are somewhat sparse, presumably because nothing much happened. I had given up my useless strategy of coping with attacks of agonising anxiety by *gritting my teeth and carrying on*. But I had no alternative plan, apart from simply hoping that things might get better one day, when I got older. Increasingly, however, I wished that I would magically cease to exist, making it all unnecessary.

Unfortunately, wishing for things is equally useless, and in reality I was deteriorating into a clinical depression. A clinically inclined observer would have noted my social withdrawal, some loss of appetite, sleep disturbance with early waking, loss of my usual interests and motivations, and a low and worried mood. Basically I was hiding away in my room and hardly speaking to any of the family. I was lying on my bed a lot but occasionally sneaking downstairs for a bit of food, taking it back upstairs to eat.

At the time I would not have recognised this as an illness or disorder. I was simply having a rest from that terrible anxiety. My insomnia did not worry me, as it had a positive aspect. As mentioned previously, one of my hobbies was long-distance radio listening, and if I was awake in the early hours I could hear some of the North American stations coming through on Medium Wave. St. Johns in Newfoundland was always the strongest signal, but occasionally there were glimpses of stations around Boston and New York. These weren't special overseas broadcasts; they were the ordinary stations that local American or Canadian people would hear. The wavering quality of these weak signals, struggling all the way across the Atlantic, evoked an image of them bouncing across the waves of the ocean. Even in the midst of depression, I had a feeling of wonderment at this contact with a land so far away.

But then it changed to a feeling of sadness. Strangely my mind went to my Uncle George, wondering if he had ever listened to these stations when he was over there. George was my father's younger brother, and during the Second World War he had served in the Merchant Navy. He had become ill on ship and was taken to hospital in New York, but died there. A few years afterwards I was named after him, and later on I was told the story, so I did feel a connection. My father was always sad that he never found out exactly what had happened to his brother, or where he was buried.

My introverted character undoubtedly helped me to survive this year of self-imposed solitary confinement in my room. My needs were few. There was a single bed covered in several heavy blankets to protect against the freezing northern winters. This was before people had duvets and central heating. Being a plumber, my father had fitted a radiator in the room, but his skills had not extended to the fitting of electrical pumps, and the radiator heated up only sporadically.

Above the radiator was a small window which gave a glimpse of the bleak County Durham landscape. At night the television transmitter mast at Pontop Pike could be seen as a vertical row of red lights on the horizon. This transmitter had been built for the televising of the Queen's coronation, but my family still lacked a television set. My mother did not see any need for such things. Maybe she would buy one when they had become less expensive and more reliable. However, the presence of the red lights on the horizon gave me a point of contact with the outside world, at which I sat and gazed every night. Quite often, of course, the lights were obscured by fog or rain, and then I would stare out in the hope of being able to detect a faint glimmer of redness.

During the day, I lay on my bed and studied the picture rail. This ran around the walls of my room, a foot or so down from the ceiling. One day I was surprised to find myself flying, or hovering in mid-air, beside it. My mind told me that I was just dreaming, so I tried to put my feet on the ground to put a stop to it, but they would not reach. With delight I decided to follow this sensation, and made a little journey back and forth along beside the picture rail. It was like being in the swimming baths, hanging on to the hand-rail, but much lighter than that. These floating daydreams became quite a regular event, which I looked forward to, but I cannot remember how I made them happen. Presumably after spending hours relaxing on my bed, I was drifting off into a hypnotic state, in which floating sensations of this kind do occur. Or perhaps they were hallucinations induced by my solitary existence.

The picture rail also featured in a more disquieting experience. I had noticed a slow ticking noise coming from one short section of the rail, and after looking through a book I decided that it could be a death watch beetle. My father did not believe that our house would be harbouring anything so exotic, so the picture rail was allowed to stay on the wall. It continued to tick, and I pressed my ear to it, imagining some creature inside. I told myself that it had nothing to do with death. Over-imaginative I might have been, but not superstitious. Again, in hindsight, I do not know what was really happening here. It could have been some sort of beetle, or it could have been another type of hallucination.

Something else that I heard one day was my mother's voice, louder than usual. She was downstairs talking to my father, I think, and she was shouting *I can't stand this any longer*. At least that is what I thought she said, and I don't know what she was talking about, but I had the feeling that it referred to me, hiding in my room all this time. *Good*, I thought. I was still angry that no one seemed to know what to do about me.

One really positive skill that I discovered during this time alone was the art of daydreaming. Some people have a moral disapproval of this activity (or inactivity), and accuse you of thinking about things you should not be thinking about, and of being lazy. I remember teachers who would say *stop daydreaming* to any child who was not actively writing at his desk. But I discovered that it had a great power. While my body remained deeply relaxed on my bed, I fantasized about doing extraverted things. I started to imagine going out and facing people, without this thought automatically making me tense or worried. In my mind I found that I could do absolutely anything, and my heart would stay still and my face would stay cool.

It took me a long time, but I began to think that maybe I could try actually walking up the street. Around this time my energy seemed to revive, and I had the feeling that something was going to change. *I think I'll go and see the doctor*, I told my mother.

Imaginal desensitization is a cognitive behaviour therapy technique for the treatment of phobias or specific anxieties. It became popular in the 1960's and 70's, when it was known simply as a type of behaviour therapy (distinguishing it from purely verbal therapies such as psychotherapy or psychoanalysis). The basic idea is that if a person is repeatedly put into his feared situation, and if he takes just one small step at a time, then he will gradually get used to it. However, putting him into a real-life situation at first might be either too fear-provoking or too difficult to arrange. So then it was realised that the person could be asked instead to deliberately imagine these nervous situations, in the same gradual way, and this mental rehearsal would prepare the ground for tackling them in reality.

The person is usually first taught to do relaxation exercises, in order to be able to achieve a state of deep relaxation, during which he can better imagine his phobic situations. His relaxed state will help him to settle down from any tension produced by his imaginings.

There has been much technical debate about whether imaginal desensitization is the best way to go about the treatment of phobias, or whether it is more efficient to go straight to real-life methods, combined with principles from cognitive therapy. Also, does relaxation aid the process, or is it unnecessary? However, there is no doubt that something happens when you repeatedly imagine the things that make you nervous, as long as you do it in a positive sort of way. A relaxed physical state probably aids that. Clearly this was what I was doing, in an untutored natural sort of way, during all those months in my room. And certainly it seemed to get me moving again.

Relaxation exercises *are a popular type of behavioural therapy, perhaps less used these days, now that psychological therapy has become more cognitive. They are helpful particularly when the aim is to learn how to positively do nothing. This might be because a person is habitually and excessively active, or because they find it impossible not to react to every little event.*

In a state of relaxation you are fully conscious of yourself and your surroundings, but you have suspended any reaction to them. There are many techniques for achieving this kind of relaxation, all emphasising slightly different aspects. Examples include hypnosis, meditation, yoga, and mindfulness. Some people find these rather exotic (although for some that can increase their appeal). You might prefer a simplified and basic approach such as the Progressive Relaxation method (Jacobsen's technique):

Take fifteen minutes every evening (or whatever time of day suits you) to sit in a comfortable chair with your eyes closed (but don't fall asleep). Start with any part of the body, your arms and hands perhaps. First make them tense by either clenching them up or stretching them out, really quite hard. Then very slowly let them go, letting the tension ease out very gradually. Then do the same with the next part of your body, for example your legs and feet, then your shoulders, neck, face and forehead.

While relaxing each part of the body, let your breath become slow and easy, by breathing out slowly as you let go of tension. Finally let your whole body settle into a state of stillness and lightness, and stay like that for several minutes. Notice that you can hardly feel any part of your body now, and indeed you could almost be floating. There is absolutely no need to respond to anything (just ignore that telephone!).

Although you can do all this under your own steam, you might find it helpful to follow an audio recording of relaxation exercises. There are many types available, some with pleasant music, but preferably with the soothing voice of a therapist guiding you through the exercises.

Slow breathing exercises are another useful physical skill. Daily relaxation exercises, over a period of several weeks or months, can help to gradually lessen your general stress level. But at an actual moment of high anxiety or tension, it may be more practical to try a slow breathing technique. The principle here is that anxiety tends to give you an urge to take in more breath, but this excess of oxygen will only increase your heart rate and anxiety further. So the idea is to learn to ignore the urge to breathe excessively, and to relax by breathing less. This might seem counter-intuitive, but it really does work.

First do a test of your present breathing capacity. Take a deep breath and then let it go as slowly as you can, for as long as you can, until there is no more air to come out. Make a note of how long you were able to breathe out (count the seconds or use a watch). You should reach at least fifteen seconds, but some only manage five. The latter could indicate a severe lack of fitness or chronic asthma. Or it could reflect a habit of fast and shallow breathing (chronic hyperventilation), resulting from stress. You are now ready to start training your breathing, with the aim of improving beyond this baseline measure.

Count to ten *is wise advice, meaning that you restrain yourself from reacting immediately and emotionally to a situation. Instead you allow enough time to consider a more rational response. As an exercise, try literally counting from one to ten while breathing out slowly in one long breath (counting silently or even aloud). Try to let go of your tension by the time you get to ten. You can practise this slow breathing whenever you have a few spare minutes, in order to be ready for moments of stress when you really need it.*

19

SEEKING HELP

1963–64

One day at the age of eighteen I left the house and walked towards the doctor's surgery, which was a big old house in the middle of Wrekenton. It felt strange to be outside after such a long time in my room. The daylight seemed bright, and the air moved in a breeze against my face. In those days, very few people had a telephone to ring for a doctor's appointment, so you simply went in and reported to the receptionist. Then you sat down in one of the old wooden chairs placed around the walls of the waiting room. Your next task was to take note of the people who were already there, in order to know your place in the queue (my mother had to explain this to me, as I had never been to the doctor before on my own). I sat and waited for nearly an hour, and previously might have developed an increasing torment of anxiety (indeed some phobic people would avoid seeing a doctor simply because of anxiety about the waiting room). However, after a year of teaching myself to relax, I felt reasonably calm and was able to wait patiently.

Sitting in front of the doctor, I condensed my story down to five minutes, which seemed an appropriate length after counting the number of patients who were still waiting. Fortunately, he grasped the situation immediately, accepting what I said without criticism, and suggested that he should refer me to a psychiatrist. *Nerve specialist* was what he actually said, this being the euphemism for psychiatrists in those days (who might otherwise have been known as *loony doctors*). Having heard something on the radio about these things, I had expected him to be upfront and say *psychiatrist*. However, I didn't quibble. An appointment would arrive in about six weeks, he said, and in the meantime he would see me once more for another chat. A six week wait sounded rather tedious, I thought. Having screwed up my courage to see a doctor, I wanted to be getting on with it, rather than just going back to my room. Still, I could hardly complain, after taking a year to get round to seeking help.

So while I was waiting for this appointment, I tried to keep the momentum going. Perhaps it would help if I learned something about psychiatry before seeing the psychiatrist. *I think I'll try going into Newcastle to look for a book,* I announced to my mother. This was something I hadn't done for a long time, a clear sign that I was beginning to feel better. Going into Newcastle involved a walk up the street to the bus stop, and then a five-mile journey on the bus, across the Tyne Bridge and into the city centre. For me, this had become associated with agonies of self-consciousness and a loudly thumping heart, but I was going to do it in the middle of the day when the buses would not be crowded.

Many phobic people like to be accompanied by a trusted friend or relative when tackling an anxiety-provoking journey. The friend's presence would be reassuring (someone to take care of you in the event of a panic attack?), or perhaps their conversation would be a useful distraction from the feelings of anxiety. However, other phobic people prefer to work solo. The main advantage of this is that you have no significant witnesses to your torment. If you make a fool of yourself by going hot and sweating in front of the entire population of Newcastle, you can tell yourself that these people don't know who you are and you will never see them again. A further advantage of being on your own is that you are free to take things at your own pace, rather than being pressured by a friend who is more interested in their own shopping.

Fortunately, my journey into Newcastle went well. On the top deck of the bus, I distracted myself by looking at the view. The dull and dirty streets of Gateshead were never a pleasant sight, but at least I was seeing them again. Then there was the Tyne Bridge, with its huge arched spans of metal. It was always a great scene, with all the other bridges away to the left, and the powerful river flowing beneath.

Getting off the bus in the main street, surrounded by people coming and going, I noted my heart thumping, as expected. *Just let it thump, it's not important, no one can see how you feel*, I persuaded myself. *Isn't it great to be out free on my own!* After wandering round the quieter streets for half an hour, I was elated to find that my heart had stopped thumping. This was an ideal sequence of events. If you can make yourself stay in the anxious situation long enough to settle down, you can go home feeling successful, leading to greater confidence on the next occasion. Of course, it takes more than just one or two successes to make a cure, but these are moments of significant change.

Walking along the wide pavements of Northumberland Street, I felt reasonably calm. Then I reached the bookshop, and went through the door with a certain amount of tension. Buying a book on psychological problems is not easy for a teenager with social anxiety. When you hand it over to the girl on the till, you can imagine her wondering why you want a book like that. *He must be one of those people not right in the head*, you can hear her thinking.

There weren't actually many mental health books available

in those days, and the embarrassment of looking at them was compounded by their placement next to the section on *Witchcraft and the Occult.* I found a slim paperback entitled *New Horizons in Psychiatry.* This was the 1960's and everything was supposedly new, modern, progressive or scientific. There was optimism about the future, except of course for the threat of nuclear war and the extinction of the human race (for example the Cuban missile crisis in 1962). The ignorance of our parents' generation was being swept away by education and science, and I was totally in tune with all that. This book on psychiatry offered hope of progress. Mental illness, anxiety and depression were now well recognised by respectable experts, and there was reason to hope that they could be cured. The concept of *lunacy* had gone, and the still fashionable ideas of *psychoanalysis* were being exposed as unscientific nonsense. The new approach would involve the development of drug therapies, and there was also the promising new Behaviour Therapy. And the modern National Health Service (*the best in the world*, people said) would be in the forefront of this progress. I really looked forward to seeing a psychiatrist.

I haven't received an appointment yet, I told the doctor after six weeks had passed. *They've lost the referral letter,* he reported the following week. My optimistic view of the Health Service shrank a little. The doctor seemed embarrassed and apologetic, so I comforted him with my mother's view that *hospitals just can't be trusted.* He wondered what I meant, so I told him the story of my tonsils.

When I was about seven, a doctor had arranged for me to go into the local hospital to have my tonsils removed. After a nervous few weeks, the day arrived, and I was put through the traditional hospital admission ritual, which always involved being given a hot bath. I sat in this bath for ten minutes, thinking that it was rather hotter than usual, but perhaps that was because hospitals had better boilers than we had at home. However, the nurse then took my temperature and informed my mother that it was too high. This meant that I might be suffering from an infection, and therefore they could not operate on me. My mother felt cheated, and accused the nurse of having put me in excessively hot water. However, I was sent home somewhat deflated, but at least my tonsils have remained intact to this day. Clearly there never was any need to remove them. Is it possible that this hospital had devised a cunning plan to fight against all these unnecessary tonsillectomies demanded by medical tradition? On the other hand, maybe it really was just a blunder.

I would now have to wait a little longer to see the psychiatrist. In the end my total waiting time for a first appointment was nearly three months, and I have always remembered the feeling of helplessness that is induced by this kind of institutional slowness.

New Horizons in Psychiatry (Peter Hays 1964) is a book worth revisiting as an object lesson in our inability to judge recent progress, let alone forecast the future. Ideas regarded as progressive can become totally old-fashioned within a few decades. And changes which were confidently expected can completely fail to happen.

In 1964 it was expected that the new anti-depressant drugs would allow psychiatrists to dispense with electro-convulsive treatment (ECT). But although ECT remains as controversial as ever, it is still widely used. It is true that there is less of it now, but the reduction is nowhere near as great as predicted.

In 1964 psychiatrists were beginning to feel more respected, at least by the general public, who had stopped calling them loony doctors. But they still felt second class compared with their medical and surgical colleagues, who were proper doctors in proper hospitals. They hoped that they would acquire further respect when new psychiatric units were built within general hospitals, and that this would attract greater numbers of higher quality professionals into the career of psychiatry. Whether this has actually happened is still a matter of debate.

In 1964 psychiatrists felt that psychotherapy for neurosis should be an essential part of their work, but at the same time there would never be enough time to do it, as they were obliged to give priority to major psychotic illness rather than neurosis (which was regarded as a less important problem). But they also felt that there was no one else to whom psychotherapeutic work could be delegated. Certainly non-medical practitioners or lay psychotherapists should not be allowed to manage patients, in case an apparent neurosis turned out to be due to a brain tumour or a psychosis, or some other medical condition. Non-doctors could not be trusted to spot real illnesses of that kind. The psychiatric profession held on to this dilemma for several decades, until other professions such as clinical psychology came along and demonstrated (eventually) that they were perfectly capable of taking care of these patients. Sometimes advances in treatment have to first overcome resistance from the restrictive practices of a long established profession.

Telling your story *is a major part of any psychological therapy. A skilled listener or therapist will help by guiding you in the right direction, preventing you from being diverted by irrelevant matters. But ultimately it is your responsibility to be clear and accurate. Don't cover up the bits that embarrass you. These might be the most important part of the story. And don't cover up for other people. If your spouse or other relative has made your life a misery, say so. There is no place here for diplomatic loyalty. At the same time, don't neglect to mention important facts where you yourself might be at fault.*

Telling the full story will be therapeutic in various ways. It helps you think more clearly. Having to explain things to someone else is a good way of explaining them to yourself. Talking about a problem can help you stand back and look at it with greater objectivity. Or an emotional release may be triggered by speaking openly about events that you have been suppressing.

20

THE MENTAL HOSPITAL

1964

My appointment arrived at last. The psychiatrist turned out to be a woman, but she did not introduce herself and this left me unsure of her profession. With the gender assumptions of the day, I had presumed that all doctors or psychiatrists would be male, so maybe she was a nurse or social worker. Anyway, I did not mind who she was, if she could get me sorted out. She asked the usual questions about symptoms, the history of the problem, and general family background. This time I got a full half hour to tell my story, which seemed luxurious. *It'll be best if you come into hospital for some treatment,* she concluded. *I'll arrange it for this Friday.* Having read the book about the wonderful new horizons in psychiatry, I had no hesitation about this. I was looking forward to whatever treatment they could devise for me.

At this stage I had no idea where the mental hospital was. My mother had sometimes mentioned Sedgefield, south of Durham, as a fearful place where some unfortunate people were sent. The old Victorian asylums tended to be known by the name of their nearest village. But I assumed that I would be going to somewhere more modern, like the book had described, perhaps in a leafy suburb of Newcastle. However, it turned out that the unfortunate residents of Gateshead had to go to St. Mary's Hospital, near Stannington, fifteen miles north in the wilds of the Northumberland countryside. A male social worker arrived in his car to take me there. I took with me my book about new horizons in psychiatry, in case I needed to study it. For some reason I was expecting my treatment to be clever and intellectual in nature.

On arrival, my bag was searched for sharp implements or other dangerous things. If you had a razor, even an electric one, they took it away and you had to ask to borrow it every morning. As I had yet to start shaving, this problem did not arise for me. The only dangerous thing in my bag was my book on psychiatry. It was examined suspiciously. *We don't like things like that lying around*, the charge nurse said, albeit apologetically. *Just ask for it whenever you want to read it*, he said, putting it in his drawer.

Next, my admission was completed with the traditional ritual of a hospital bath (*it's because we get some people coming in with fleas and lice*), during which my clothes were taken away and put in a locked store cupboard, leaving me with just my pyjamas. I was shown to my bed, where I was to rest for the weekend. This was in the middle of a long row of beds, in a narrow dormitory. Pictures of wartime military hospitals or TB sanatoriums remind me of it.

My bed faced the toilet. *Ask us if you want to go to the toilet*, said the charge nurse, implying that they would be obliged to keep an eye on me if I did. There would be no difficulty in keeping an eye on me, as the toilet door was like a stable door, with the top half missing. Presumably you could be observed hanging yourself. The bottom half of the door provided some modesty if you were sitting down. The charge nurse was apologetic again. *Don't worry, you'll get used to it. No one looks.*

Suddenly I noticed that there were no other patients. I was entirely alone in this long row of beds. *They've all gone home on leave for the weekend*, it was explained, and I was relieved that it was going to be so peaceful. It seemed strange to be tucked up in a hospital bed, though. I don't know why that was done. Presumably it was just another nursing tradition. They established their professional relationship with patients by putting them to bed.

There was nothing to do while lying there in bed, so I was glad when a meal arrived. It was ham with salad, but mainly I remember the large quantity of beetroot. Fortunately I really liked beetroot. It was one of the things that my father grew in our garden, and my mother always had jars of it pickled in vinegar. So I ate the meal quite happily, taking care not to stain the bedclothes with purple beetroot juice. *That was quite nice,* I thought, *I wonder what they'll give me later.* When the evening meal arrived, it was exactly the same, including the beetroot. But that was fine. I assumed that they had opened a jar of beetroot and just wanted to finish it up.

Next morning, fried eggs and bacon arrived, plus lots and lots of beetroot. I ate it happily enough, but the beetroot was beginning to seem weird. *Perhaps it's a treatment*, it dawned upon me. This was a daft idea, of course, but you must remember that I had been reading about advances in modern psychiatry. Somewhere I had read a theory about certain foods having therapeutic benefit, and perhaps now I was in the hands of clever doctors who had discovered that beetroot healed the mind. At the very least they must be doing research on it, and I was a guinea pig. *Wait a minute, this place is out in the backwoods of Northumberland, so that's not very likely*, I cautioned myself. Perhaps they just had a mountain of beetroot in the kitchen stores. I decided it would be unwise to ask.

It was Saturday, and the charge nurse had disappeared off for the weekend. A new male nurse (man in white coat) appeared, and took up a position leaning against the wall facing the end of my bed. He said nothing, but just looked at me and kept on looking. And then he combed his hair. These were the days of rock and roll, when young men stood around combing their hair, posing like their heroes in the movies. I turned my head on the pillow and pretended to be asleep. But after an hour or two of this, with him just standing there looking at me, it began to feel quite threatening. I felt a rising fear taking hold of me, a real fear, not just my usual anxiety about being looked at. *What was he doing? What was he going to do?*

Again I tried to be positive. *Perhaps this is a treatment.* Maybe he had read my file, and was trying to do some behaviour therapy, as mentioned in the book on psychiatry. By looking at me in this prolonged way, he was trying to get me used to it. But then I had a more sinister thought. Perhaps he was an evil bully who looked through patients' files to find out how best to torment them with their worst fears. He was trying to provoke me with all this silent staring, and then when I broke down he would be able to deny doing anything. Now that I had worked this out, I could defeat him. But I was afraid. I remembered that my clothes had been taken away, and for the moment I was a prisoner. He kept on staring and combing his hair. I kept on pretending to be paying no attention. *Don't show your fear to him. Just hang on until there is a chance of escape.*

Lunch arrived. There was more beetroot. This time I ate it grimly. Two o'clock came, visiting time, and my parents arrived on the hospital bus. *I've got to get out of here*, I pleaded, explaining about the nurse and being imprisoned in bed. They looked around warily, not accustomed to such situations. My father looked angry. They had been sceptical about my readiness to go into a lunatic asylum. They had not read my book on new horizons in psychiatry.

My mother disappeared off to the ward office, returning with a nurse and my clothes. *We'll take him home on the bus*, she over-ruled the nurse. *But he's only been here for a day*, he protested. *And that's quite long enough,* I thought, but I did not say anything. Escape was the first priority.

The three of us got on the hospital bus. *There are more leaving than there were coming,* remarked the driver, checking whether my escape was authorised. My mother reassured him: *It's all right, he's with us.* We were silent all the way home, and I returned to my room with a feeling of overwhelming misery.

The sociology of asylums was studied by Erving Goffman in the USA in the 1950's, by going undercover as an employee of a mental hospital in Washington (Goffman 1961). He saw similarities between mental hospitals and other institutions such as prisons, concentration camps, monasteries, orphanages and military organizations. Total institutions are places of residence and work where a large number of individuals are cut off from wider society for a period of time. There is a fundamental split between a large managed group (the inmates), and a small supervisory staff. Human needs are handled in a bureaucratic and impersonal way. Upon entering the institution, processes are set in motion to destroy the inmate's old self and create a new self. The inmate learns that, if and when he gets out of the institution, life on the outside will never be quite what it was before.

Some writers have argued that Goffman's views were exaggerated or one-sided, and that mental hospitals were seldom as bad as he described. However, Goffman claimed that he had to present a partisan view in order to describe things as the patient might experience them.

Waving a magic wand is what you hope that an expert doctor or psychologist or hospital will do for you. In my case the present day magic wands were not available, which is why an admission to hospital (as opposed to outpatient treatment) was required. The naïve patient (like me) imagines that the doctors will make a clever diagnosis of his condition, and then will apply a clever treatment which will make him feel ever so much better. For example, you hope that a drug or medicine *will do the trick. No effort required, you simply take a pill and wait to feel better. Is this kind of magic really possible? Well yes, sometimes it is, in some situations. The hard work of cognitive behavioural therapy is not always the answer to everything.*

Some people are very wary of medication for stress or depression, because they have heard all sorts of scare stories about side effects and addiction. There is truth in some of these stories, but beware of exaggerations.

Other people regard pills as a sign of moral inadequacy. They think they should just pull themselves together. In fact it is perfectly logical to try out a physical treatment to see if it can counteract the physical symptoms of stress or depression. The only real questions are whether this approach does have the required effect, and whether it is safe.

You should feel free to take advantage of this useful tool, especially if other methods are either not available or not successful. It can help to keep your life going while you try to tackle the basic causes of your problem. Just don't expect it to solve the problem by itself. You also have to work on it, for example with psychotherapy, cognitive behavioural therapy, or just common sense.

The main types of modern medication for stress problems are Tranquillizers (including sleeping tablets) and Anti-depressants. The former have a rapid calming effect, and can become addictive, so it is better to use them only for short periods, or intermittently. Anti-depressants are slower-acting and not addictive. They need at least two or three weeks to start working fully. If the first prescription does not work, you can try an alternative type.

21

MIGHT AS WELL GIVE UP

1964

My escape from the asylum did not last long. I was absolutely deflated now. After starting to make progress through my own efforts, and after being led to believe that modern psychiatry had something to offer, all this had been taken away by my admission to Stannington.

I might as well kill myself. That was the only possible move left now. Back in my room after returning from the hospital, I knew what had to be done. I had considered this before, and knew it wasn't easy. One afternoon some time ago, I had wired myself up to an electrical plug and pushed it into a socket in my bedroom. For a minute or two I had hesitated over pressing down the switch. But I was too afraid. It might be very painful, because it might not work fully and I would simply end up with burns. Indeed it might set fire to the house.

The best thing would be an overdose of drugs. I had read in the newspapers about such suicides, and I had also read my mother's favourite murder mysteries, in which the victim would die rapidly after being poisoned with something like cyanide or strychnine. So, after my parents had gone to bed, I crept downstairs to investigate the medicine cabinet. There was a full bottle of aspirin, but nothing else. *That'll do,* I decided. I had no knowledge of drugs or medicines, but my mother had always warned that taking more than one or two aspirins could be dangerous. A whole bottle would surely be fatal.

There were fifty tablets. I poured out some orange drink and diluted it with water. My experience of taking pills was very limited, and strangely it never occurred to me that they could be swallowed whole. My mother always recommended chewing them up with a bit of bread. That was her personal method of getting them down. So I sat at my bedroom table with fifty tablets laid out, chewing them one by one. A sip of orange washed each one down, but the horribly bitter taste grew and grew, until I became quite daunted by this task. With relief I managed to swallow the last one, and settled into bed, looking forward to being dead in the morning.

Two hours later I woke up feeling sick, so I found a bowl and sat vomiting the contents of my stomach into it over the next hour or so. The next morning I confessed what I had done. *Oh, I thought I heard something in the night*, said my mother. The doctor came and sent for an ambulance (in those days the public were discouraged from calling an ambulance themselves, but doctors were more available for urgent home visits).

I was taken to Bensham General Hospital to have my stomach washed out (a large amount of aspirin can be quite harmful, even if not fatal). A young female nurse came and glared at me through the doorway of the room where I was lying. She muttered some comment about *these time-wasters*, and stormed off. However, by this time I really did not care. *They can do or say whatever they like.* So the nurse dealing with me was quite surprised at my calmness while she slid a tube down my throat, filled my stomach with water, and then syphoned it out again. *Some people struggle. You were very good*, she said, confirming that not all nurses were nasty.

Afterwards I lay in bed feeling resigned to whatever happened next. But there was also a glimmer of having achieved something. I had faced and accepted the idea of death. I was content to die. Nothing could be worse than that, surely. I could now face life with a greater degree of detachment. Actually I felt rather numb.

You'll have to go back to the mental hospital, they said. No problem. I had a new attitude. The social worker arrived to take me back to the wilds of Northumberland. *You will have to stay in this time. You've been put on a Section, which means you cannot leave for 28 days,* he explained. *Was there any particular reason why you left the hospital at the weekend?* I described the silently staring and combing nurse, and somehow he didn't seem too surprised. *I did wonder if it was wise to take you in that day. They usually don't admit anyone at weekends,* he apologized.

Smiling *tells other people that you are friendly, sympathetic or caring, and they smile in return. Or it can simply express a happy feeling, and some of this will spread to other people. I had always been a smiley person, finding it easier than words and very effective in disarming hostility. But in my downward descent from anxiety to depression, I had stopped smiling. Not only had I lost all happiness, I had stopped caring for anything or anyone, including myself.*

When people make comments about someone who has committed suicide, they sometimes wonder how this person could have gone ahead and hurt those who care for him. But they are overlooking the possibility that the person did not believe that anyone cared for him, and in any case he no longer cared for them or for anything else.

Health workers' attitudes towards attempted suicides *vary considerably (much like the general population). It has sometimes been found that general hospital staff can be quite hostile and unsympathetic to the typical overdose case. They might regard attempted suicide as immoral and meriting punishment. Or they* might use pseudo-psychiatric ideas to describe these patients as merely attention-seeking. General hospital nurses and physicians are less likely than psychiatrists to regard the patient as suffering from genuine depression, or as having a serious wish to die (Platt and Salter 1987).

There is a huge variation in professional attitudes within each profession, so it is unwise to make generalisations. However, it is clear that there is still work to be done in altering unhelpful or prejudiced attitudes.

Bad nurses are only a very small minority of the nursing profession. Even in the old days, before rigorous selection and detailed training, most mental health nurses were kind and decent people, which is a very good basis for professional skills. However, the occasional bad nurse can do a lot of harm, and therefore the profession spends a lot of time on maintaining and improving its standards. A report by Hamilton (2010) provides a good outline of these issues.

Even general hospital nurses need to be trained in basic mental health awareness. This should include an understanding of the links between physical and mental health, and also knowledge of the side-effects associated with psychiatric medication.

For nurses on psychiatric wards, training in both listening and observation is important. Nurses must recognise the usefulness of spending time with patients on the ward. Training should include contact with service users and carers who can give their own expert insight into their experience of mental health problems. This will help the nurse to see the person and not just the condition.

All of this should apply not just to the established ward staff, but also to temporary or agency staff. Candidates for nursing training need to be carefully assessed for any negative attributes which may prove resistant to change. Sometimes you just have to accept that leopards do not change their spots.

Other organisational, structural or cultural problems need to be addressed, of course. The management of the ward or wider hospital can sometimes become toxic, adversely affecting the performance of individual nurses.

22

BACK IN STANNINGTON

1964

I arrived back at the mental hospital. The charge nurse was on duty again, and after asking about the staring and combing nurse, he looked embarrassed. *We can't get enough decent staff,* he confessed. *Sometimes at weekends they send over these nurses from the back wards, and they haven't got a clue.* Briefly I contemplated these back wards, wondering what kind of purgatory they might contain. They would be for the long stay patients, those who were really out of their minds. But not to worry, at least I wasn't in there. I was in the part of the hospital where patients went home again. Indeed, most of them went home every weekend.

Actually it was not too bad, for its day. In some ways it was preferable to one of today's acute admission wards, where bed numbers have been cut to the bone, and the pressures can be frantic. In those days there was plenty of space and no hurry. Of course, I should not have been in hospital at all, if I had got some earlier help as an out-patient. But I do not know whether such facilities were available then (and you might sometimes question this even now). However, given that I did end up in an old mental hospital, the treatment and care was actually quite reasonable. Indeed I may have escaped some of the excesses of the subsequent decade, when thousands of anxious and depressed patients were given enthusiastic doses of benzodiazepine tranquillizers, becoming addicted to them for many years afterwards.

In 1964 very few pharmaceutical treatments were available, so my first option was a course of ECT (electro-convulsive therapy) for depression. I agreed to this quite happily, having read about it in my book on modern psychiatry, and getting the impression that it could be something of a magic wand. ECT has had a very bad press over the years, but I have to say that it did produce a clearly positive effect on me, and as far as I know it did me no harm. For any reader who is not familiar with ECT, you go to a clinical room where you lie on a medical bed. You are given a small dose of general anaesthetic in your arm, as if you are going to have a simple brief surgical operation. While you are asleep, the psychiatrist touches your temples with a couple of electrodes which deliver a small electrical shock to the head and brain. This induces a slight fit, like an epileptic seizure, so that the body will jerk somewhat. You are unaware of all this, of course, and the worst that should happen is a mild hangover when you wake up.

The effect of my first ECT was surprisingly exciting. My whole body felt totally relaxed, and in particular something had happened to my face. For years it had held itself stiff in its attempt to hide my anxiety from the watching public, but now this tension had completely melted away. This was an extraordinary sensation, and I rushed to the bathroom to find a mirror to see what had happened to my face. *My face looks all right*, I marvelled. However, even as I watched my face in the mirror, I could feel this effect dissolving slightly. But I reassured myself that further treatments would consolidate this magic. I had now glimpsed a normality that was lost years ago, and knew now that the sickness could be driven away. Optimism had returned.

The psychiatrist asked how I had got on with the first ECT, and I told him that it made me feel as if I was ten years old again. He laughed, thinking that he could start selling the idea of ECT as a rejuvenating treatment. What I actually meant was that the age of ten was the last time I had felt that good. During my teenage years I must have grown miserably tense, gradually and imperceptibly accumulating a huge load. The ECT had suddenly lightened that load, giving a feeling of tremendous relief.

So now the treatment plan was to have twelve ECT's, at a rate of two per week. As the weeks passed, I became aware that the initial effect was not being repeated, although much of the lift from the first treatment was still there. The psychiatrist encouraged me to carry on and finish the course, and I was happy to do so. He did not know that I had developed an illicit taste for the anaesthetic, and actually looked forward to each session. If you are old enough to have had a general anaesthetic fifty years ago, you might know what I mean. In those days, when the injection was being pushed into your arm, there was a period of several seconds during which it took effect, unlike the quickness of modern anaesthetics. During those few seconds, there was a passing out sensation, which felt as if you were free-falling in a downward spiral towards infinity. Some people would find this frightening, of course, but others might enjoy it like the thrill of a roller-coaster ride. I learned to enjoy those few moments of free-fall, but I kept this secret from the psychiatrists. I knew that they would not approve.

When not having ECT, all patients went to Occupational Therapy (OT). We sat at large tables, doing various crafts such as the now-despised basket weaving. Noticing some rug making going on, I chose this, having enjoyed it as a young child at primary school. After a few weeks, however, I was totally bored, and I wondered whether to volunteer to work on the hospital farm and get out into the fresh air. Another patient pointed out that it was winter outside: *Why would you want to go out there all day, getting cold and wet, doing work for them for nothing?* He said he had worked for years digging trenches for the water company, and was very familiar with the misery of hard labour, bad weather and low pay. He blamed his job for the fact that he was now in a mental hospital. I was left with the feeling that it would be a betrayal of the other patients, and the working class in general, if I did any unpaid work for the benefit of the hospital authority. Next morning, the charge nurse was not too surprised that I had thought better of it. I returned to the tedium of Occupational Therapy, and never saw the farm where all that beetroot had come from.

One afternoon I was brought to see a different psychiatrist. *He does psychotherapy*, explained the nurse. This was something else that I had read about in the book about new horizons in psychiatry, so I was expecting something rather grand and clever, like psychoanalysis perhaps. But no, he said we would *just have a chat*. Over the weeks, we had several of these chats, and they were not very long, but I did look forward to them. Being able to talk about myself, in a common sense sort of way, was a new experience for me. So I was really disappointed one week when he did not turn up. The nurses said that he didn't have enough time that week, but in fact he never came again. Perhaps he was a trainee on temporary secondment.

After a couple of months in the hospital, they started to send me home at weekends (*on leave*). The little hospital bus took most of the patients on the ward back to Gateshead on Friday afternoons, and picked us up on Sunday afternoons for the return journey. Whenever you got on that bus you were hit by the smell of cigarettes. As soon we were moving, a great fog of smoke arose from every passenger (except me). These weren't the modern filter cigarettes. Everyone on the bus smoked Woodbines, a popular brand from wartime, cheap and strong. They were the cigarette equivalent of my father's smelly pipe.

So there I was, travelling fifteen miles back and forth to the lunatic asylum, roaming through the wilds of Northumberland on a bus full of smoke. It occurred to me that if I could do something as weird as that, then really I could do anything. Going away to University would surely not be any worse. This realisation in fact was a very useful by-product of my admission to hospital. I had acquired experience in going away from home, and had overcome some of my fears about travelling. I had sat at hospital dining tables and eaten my meals with other patients. Nothing terrible had happened. It had worked as a kind of desensitisation.

After three months in hospital, I told the psychiatrists that I was planning to resume my education. They sent me home for a couple of weeks with a supply of Largactil (Chlorpromazine), a strong tranquillizer. This was something I had not tried before, and I was disappointed to find that they just made me feel unpleasantly tired. When I reported that I had given them up, and felt better without any medication, the psychiatrists looked a bit disconcerted. However, they seemed very pleased that their efforts generally had paid off, and I was given my discharge back to the normal world again. I still had more work to do, of course, but it was up to me now.

Electro-convulsive therapy has a very bad public image these days, deriving from fears about having electric shocks delivered to your brain, and reports of patients in old institutions being punished with it. Criticisms of ECT (it causes some memory impairment, and no one really knows how it works) have been regularly reported in the press, causing many people to assume that it is an out-of-date treatment which is no longer used. On the contrary, it is still widely used by psychiatrists who find that there is no effective alternative in certain cases (Fink 2009). They argue that the technique has been much refined and side-effects are minimal.

In the UK the National Institute for Clinical Excellence has given guidelines for the use of ECT in cases of depression. It should be given only to achieve rapid and short-term improvement of severe symptoms, after other treatment options have failed or when the condition is considered life-threatening. The risks of ECT should be taken into account especially in elderly people, in children and adolescents, and during pregnancy.

For less severe cases of depression it is usually recommended now that the patient should receive cognitive behavioural therapy and/or antidepressant medication. CBT was not available in 1964, and although some antidepressant drugs were appearing, they tended to have quite bad side effects. Nowadays there is a wide range of antidepressants, but unfortunately the availability of CBT can still be rather patchy.

Exploration, at a personal level, simply means trying out various things to see what happens. We each have our own horizon, beyond which there are unfamiliar ideas and experiences. As you go through life, this horizon usually expands, but sometimes it can shrink. For example, when we are suffering from stress or depression we become less willing to go to new places or try new things. But eventually there is no choice: you have to progress or die.

You have to recognise that a change is necessary. This means a real necessity, not just boredom or a passing fancy. Then you need courage and persistence in the face of the inevitable problems. And finally you need to know when to stop and consolidate. There is always a limit on the pace of change. You have to make some use of what you have discovered, before moving on to the next thing.

Seeking out your fears requires an exploratory attitude. If you have *a phobia or nervousness about something, the natural tendency is to avoid going anywhere near it. Common phobias include crowds of people, shops, enclosed places, heights, travelling by bus, train or plane, and specific things such as insects, snakes or other animals. Some phobias develop from actual traumatic events, and others are picked up from other people (such as parents).*

Take agoraphobia as an example. This is nervousness triggered by going out of your home and into public places such as shops or transport (or even by just thinking about doing so). The physical and mental feelings of anxiety are deeply unpleasant, and it is not surprising if you try to find reasons not to go out. The trouble is, the longer you stay at home, the harder it gets. You are stuck between a rock and a hard place.

Now you need the cognitive behavioural technique known as desensitisation or graded exposure. This means putting yourself in your feared situation, not heroically but in a gradual and planned sort of way, enabling you to get used to easier versions of the situation first, before moving on the harder ones. Along the way, you learn that your nervousness does lessen with time and exploration, and that each success leads to further success. You have reversed the previous situation where each failure led to the next failure.

People sometimes seek out therapy with the idea that something will be done for them. But cognitive behavioural therapy clearly has to be done by you, even if you are being guided and encouraged by a therapist. You actively seek out an anxiety-provoking experience and make it an experiment. You will try it and see what happens.

23

FREEDOM

1964

Out of hospital, at the age of nineteen, I discovered that I could recommence my A-level studies at Newcastle College of Further Education in the autumn. In the meantime I had several months to wait, which was a bit frustrating, as I was aware that I was now three years behind in the educational rat race. But maybe I could use this time to learn some other sorts of lessons.

First I went to the Employment Exchange (as it was called in those days), and registered as unemployed, in order to claim unemployment benefit *(the dole)*. I was still feeling somewhat guilty about being a financial burden on my mother, and at least I could give her this bit of money. She was rather uneasy about me going to the Employment Exchange. As a working class conservative with experience of the 1930's, she regarded *being on the dole* as a social disgrace, the reserve of idle scroungers. I tried to persuade her that it was a perfectly normal aspect of modern socialist society, and in any case I would not be on it for long. Besides, they might even find me a job, although this seemed unlikely, especially as I had told them that I had just come out of the mental hospital.

I was beginning to free myself from my guilt about not paying my way. Without that freedom it would be impossible to go to college or university, where I would have to depend on support from either my parents or the state. I was also getting used to the idea of doing things that no one else in the family had ever done. After being the first to go into a mental hospital, and then the first to go on the dole, I would follow that up by being the first to go to university. How's that for social class mobility!

Going to the Employment Exchange and standing in the dole queue was a good exercise in getting out into the world beyond my bedroom. In addition, at least once per week I got on a bus and made the journey into Newcastle city centre, just to wander round the shops or have a cup of tea in a cafe. Otherwise I felt I could easily lose my newly found confidence, and become anxious again. Going to college in Newcastle would require a daily bus journey, as well as eating in the students' canteen, so it was vital to keep my phobia at bay.

In the meantime I pondered about what had caused my anxiety to develop. Previously I had been rather ashamed of my embarrassment. Perhaps normal teenagers all became self-conscious, but then were strong enough to shrug it off, whereas I was some sort of psychological weakling. But I had now survived several rather tough experiences, probably beyond the worst nightmares of most of my peers, so the psychological weakling theory just did not stand up.

I wondered what other explanation there might be. Had I suffered some kind of traumatic event in early childhood, which had twisted my mind? Books on psychology from the library were mainly psychoanalytic in their theories, and suggested that you can be affected by things that you have forgotten, repressed, or kept in your unconscious mind. Perhaps I could identify my demons from the past by using the hypnotic relaxation skills that I had discovered during my isolation phase. If I could get myself hypnotised enough to float, surely I could reach back into the mists of my past? However, I seemed to have lost my ability to go hypnotic, and the best I could manage was an ordinary relaxed state.

It was then that I managed to recall the incident when, as a toddler, I wandered away on the beach at Whitley Bay, and ended up being stared at in the Lost Children's Shelter. Presumably I was frightened at that time, although I could not recall the fear. It is possible to speculate that this experience could have been traumatic, and that it could have laid the foundations of a social phobia. However, this theory did not really convince me. It might have been a small part of the jigsaw, but it didn't feel helpful.

I was much more convinced by my next idea. This did not require any feats of memory, or esoteric theories. The events were still going on in front of my eyes and more especially my ears. After all these years, my mother was still denigrating and nagging at my long-suffering father. The psychological stench from this was totally obvious. Why had I not noticed it before? Presumably it was because I had never known anything different. But having now been to a place where it did not happen (the *asylum*), I could see the abnormality and toxicity of my mother's onslaught.

Previously I had colluded with her opinions, leading me to feel that my father was an embarrassment. But now I rebelled, and began to see this as wrong. Even if some of the things she said about him were true, it was evil to say them so often and with such venom. And to keep on repeating them all this time was just bitter and twisted. Suddenly I realised that the things she said about my father were the thoughts that came into my head when I felt anxious about other people scrutinising me. This was the best eureka moment I had experienced for a long time, even better than finding solutions to complex mathematical problems. I opened up my notebook and drew a line down the centre of the page. On the left hand side of the line I wrote a list of her sayings about my father, and on the right hand side I listed what I imagined people to be thinking about me. *They matched! QED.* Obviously my mind was just regurgitating this poison that I had heard so many times from my mother's mouth.

From listening to my mother I had absorbed and further developed some incorrect generalisations and assumptions about people. *People can just look at you and know what sort of person you are, and what you are thinking or feeling. And of course they will be especially interested in all your faults.*

It was suddenly obvious that a child or teenager would be disturbed by all this. *It's my mother's fault,* was my thrilled conclusion. I had found her out, like a detective in one of those murder stories she was always reading. But did she actually intend the meanings that I had absorbed from what she said? Was she even in control of her own tongue? A few years later, as a psychology student in possession of a tape recorder, I tried to test this out by recording her in full onslaught against my father. When I played this back to them, she seemed shocked for a moment, and then said *that's not me.* She was only concerned with the fact that she had a Geordie accent and did not recognise her own voice.

But in the meantime I saw no point in trying to challenge my mother, and simply decided to take revenge on her in my own mind. I would stop feeling guilty about being a financial burden on her. *She can pay for me to go to college.* I felt my heart harden in a most satisfying manner.

Suddenly a telegram summoned me to the Employment Exchange. In those days telephones were owned only by the rich or professional classes, so if a message was urgent it was delivered to your door by a man on a motorbike. A job had come up which would last for two weeks, ideal for students on their summer vacation. A dozen university students were recruited, and I was included. A factory had closed down for the annual fortnight's holiday, and the machines needed to be cleaned. The wages were surprisingly good, so I accepted readily. I was in the mood to try anything.

Something extraordinary then happened. On the first morning, while walking down the hill to the factory on the Trading Estate, I suddenly felt exhilarated. Probably it was just a feeling of unaccustomed wellbeing, all my anxiety and depression having completely disappeared. The peak of this feeling lasted for less than an hour, and it never happened again quite so extremely. For months afterwards I pondered over the details of that morning, trying to work out how to make it happen again.

Perhaps it was just the sunshine. This was the first thing I had noticed as I walked down the hill towards the Team Valley Trading Estate. It was a beautiful cool morning in the middle of summer, and the sky was entirely clear and blue. That alone was unusual. Those who say that the sun was always shining during their childhood must have lived in the South. My personal (depressed?) recollection of the North-East is of permanent cloud, fog, smog or rain. If the sun appeared at all, we did not know what to do with it.

So the heavens were heavenly. But that was almost insignificant compared with my excitement when I realized that I had become invisible. I was walking down this narrow road, and people were walking towards me and going past *without taking any notice.* It was as if they were looking straight through me. This was marvellous. I wondered if it could be due to my style of clothes. Realising that I was going to be cleaning dirty machines, I had put on my oldest shirt and trousers. I carried an old rucksack containing my sandwiches and flask of tea (my *bait*). In fact I felt a bit like my father, albeit without the old-fashioned overalls. It had crossed my mind that I would feel embarrassed to look so slovenly in public, but now I realised that *slovenly was good*. It was like camouflage, fitting in with how everyone else looked. I was no longer a grammar school boy in a blazer.

Another helpful factor in my elation might have been the simple act of doing a two mile walk down this pleasant semi-rural lane. Previously I had found a lot of benefit from going for long walks, but that was only during the dark winter evenings, when no one could see me striding along puffing and sweating. I used to walk for several miles around the Team Valley Trading Estate, always being amused by the De La Rue *money factory*, with its guard at the front door. After coming back from such a walk, I would feel quite relaxed and somehow satisfied. So the addition of a beautiful summer's morning made the experience even more pleasant.

At home that evening, I could not resist telling my mother my great discovery about invisibility. *When you're in your working clothes, people take no notice of you. They only look at you if you're dressed up.* She had no idea what I was trying to say. *You're just imagining it,* she said. After that I gave up trying to explain anything to her. She didn't want to know. I was free to be myself.

Exercise might appear to have no relevance to psychological problems or mental health, but in fact you should never forget its great effectiveness as a mood enhancer and relaxant. It is so simple, and yet so often overlooked.

What sort of exercise is suitable? Preferably it should be something that you enjoy, so that you will persist with it. And of course it needs to be readily available. Some people enjoy vigorous sports or work-outs at the gym. Others prefer the freedom of going for a walk, which costs nothing and gives you the pleasure of landscape and the open air. Or you might enjoy dancing, which provides social contact and the stimulation of music. And of course there is swimming, which gives a pleasant sensation of weightlessness and immersion. The aim should be to enjoy these activities, and to feel fitter for doing them, but not to become fanatical or competitive.

Accusing means identifying someone else's behaviour as the cause of your problems. Such an accusation does not need to be made openly, as it is more important for you to think it through, quietly and rationally, and then act to protect yourself. Your assessment needs to be a correct one, of course. False or exaggerated accusations will not solve anything, and indeed will cause further problems. Correctly identifying someone as harmful requires you first to define clearly and objectively their problem behaviour. Ask yourself whether you might be misunderstanding or misinterpreting it? Is your evidence clear and objective? Does anyone else agree with you? If you are sure about all this, you must do something about it. You can try challenging the person to change their behaviour, but often this is not possible and all you can do is to remove yourself from their influence.

Forgiveness is often thought to be a religious or moral concept. However, it has long been suggested that it is also good for your health, compared with the pernicious effects of prolonged hostility and thoughts of revenge. After freeing myself from my mother's influence, I was able to relax and see her behaviour in another light. She had probably meant no harm. It was all derived in turn from her own problems, whatever they were. No one had helped her with those.

Forgiveness does not mean that you make a friend of your enemy. That could be foolish, especially if he is still your enemy. Rather, it means that you cushion your hostility by trying to understand him better as a fellow human being.

Various steps towards forgiveness have been suggested. First realise that your hatred harms no one other than yourself, and that it ties you for ever to the person who has caused you pain. Forgiveness *enables you to start walking away. A silver lining might be found, such as the fact that you have become a better person because of whatever you have suffered. Finally, see if you can tell the story from the other person's perspective. This takes a huge effort of imagination. You have to remember that the other person will not see it your way, and must have made some other sense of it, no matter how mad, bad or stupid that might have been.*

Privacy *is the acceptable face of dishonesty. You are simply covering up things that are nobody's business but yours. It is very important for a child to learn that this is possible, otherwise he will be terrified by the idea that his mind is on public show.*

The concept of privacy includes an assortment of human needs. For example there is modesty, in the sense of keeping certain parts of the body, as well as intimate activities, hidden from public view. There is also anonymity, where you wish to remain unnoticed and unidentified in the public domain. And finally there is secrecy, which involves withholding or covering up information, if necessary by lying about it. Remember that no one has a right to see inside your head, no matter what pressure or emotional blackmail they exert upon you.

As a teenager I tended to slip into a self-conscious feeling (or unspoken assumption) that anyone could see inside my head, just by looking. This wasn't something that I had consciously pinpointed, let alone questioned. Perhaps to some extent it is a normal hang-over from infancy (before you learn to talk, you rely on your mother being able to see what you want).

So when it dawned upon me that no one could actually see inside my embarrassment and panic, this was a wonderful relief. But also humbling: why had I not known this before? Was I really that stupid and ignorant? At last I could step out into the world, confident in the knowledge that I was protected by a grown-up cloak of privacy. No one would notice if I had a moment of nervousness, and no one needed to know about all those moments that I had suffered in the past. This was different to my previous embarrassed inability to talk about these things. I knew now that I could tell people, but also knew that they wouldn't be terribly interested, so why bother?

The story finishes with me attending Newcastle College of Further Education and getting my A-level exams. I had continued to do Mathematics and Physics, because it was easier to stick with familiar subjects. But soon I realised that I was bored with all that. I was a new person now, and something different was needed. Having seen how I had solved my own psychological problems, I had the idea that it would be interesting to see what I could do for other people. Having seen the appalling ignorance that existed around mental illness, I had the idea that something should be done about it. So off I went to university to study psychology, and then clinical psychology, before starting a career as a clinical psychologist in the National Health Service in Worcestershire (Smith 2011). I never returned to the North-East.

CONCLUSION

I am grateful for the fact that I did receive some professional and medical help, and that it proved to be very useful. The general practitioner made the right diagnosis, and referred me to the correct service as available at that time. The psychiatrists also made a correct diagnosis, in terms of the medical model used by psychiatrists then and now. Then they took action to help me, first by admitting me to the psychiatric hospital, and then by giving me a course of ECT. Nowadays, the admission to hospital could be avoided, using community clinics instead. And the use of ECT would be frowned upon in cases like mine, especially at that age. The recommended treatment now would be cognitive behavioural therapy, possibly with a course of antidepressants (but only if CBT was not easily available).

But that does not mean that the older style of treatment was useless. The admission to hospital could be seen in cognitive behavioural terms firstly as a form of desensitisation, and secondly as a removal from my home environment facilitating some useful cognitive changes. These might not have been the intended results (apart from preventing suicide, it was never clear what a hospital admission was intended to achieve). Nevertheless, they were beneficial. Similarly, the ECT had a valuable effect even if it was not quite as intended, and certainly it was less risky than the addictive courses of benzodiazepines that were given later on in the 1960's and 70's.

It might appear that I am saying that I recovered *despite* the treatment, rather than because of it. This is not quite what I mean, but I do feel that the treatment helped mainly because I was somehow able to extract the right ingredients from it. This of course brings up the more general question of the degree to which a person or patient brings about his own recovery. The number of people who have overcome anxiety and depression (and all sorts of other psychological problems) is very much greater than the number of people who have received treatment of any kind (let alone the correct treatment). I am far from unique in feeling that I largely did it myself.

When treatment research trials find that some proportion of patients improve even with no treatment, this is sometimes dismissed as *spontaneous remission* due to unknown causes (such as the patient's life having taken a fortunate turn for the better). But it isn't always just luck. People actually do things to help themselves, and we would be wise to take account of this in our professional therapies.

Cognitive behaviour therapists very much recognise the active role that patients play, even when given therapy by an expert professional. Self-help can be reinforced in terms of cognitive behavioural principles, and many patients can largely do their own therapy, with a little guidance and information.

The final issue is whether people can be educated or trained in the basic skills that they need for self-help, perhaps in preparation for a time when they might have problems. Indeed, might this sort of education prevent some of these problems from developing in the first place? Both of these propositions seem fairly likely to be true. However, there is the question of which skills might need this kind of extra attention.

I would suggest that attention should be given to really basic skills, the natural things that everyone can do. Such skills are easily overlooked or neglected in normal education, as it is not appreciated how complex and interesting they can be, despite being universal. My proposed list of such skills is derived somewhat loosely from the following six pairs of opposites:

Talking – Listening (skills in communication)
Worrying – Ignoring (skills in dealing with risks)
Exploring – Keeping (skills in managing change)
Caring – Accusing (skills in relating to others)
Striving – Taking (skills in gathering resources)
Confessing – Lying (skills in achieving truth)

Readers familiar with the Five Factor theory of personality (McCrae and Costa 2003), plus a more recent sixth factor (Lee and Ashton 2005), might recognise a similarity between the above and the personality traits of Extraversion, Neuroticism, Openness, Agreeableness, Conscientiousness, and Honesty-humility. One reason for a person being poor in certain skills might be because his personality has preferred to develop the opposite ones. Society too, has preferences, and for reasons of morality or convention may approve or disapprove of certain aspects of human personality, and this will prejudice the extent to which those skills are taught or discussed. A rather more sophisticated or flexible approach to life may be required in order to achieve a healthier balance of skills.

As well as each skill itself, it is necessary to learn wisdom about how and to what extent to apply it. Each of these types of behaviour can end up being applied in a toxic manner, rather than a therapeutic or healthy one. They can be generators of problems as well as solutions for them. Learning how to apply these skills wisely can come from experience (trial-and-error), as well as from good advice. A useful general rule is to go for balance or moderation (*not too much, not too little*), but there can be times when a more extreme or definite position is called for.

Talking is a skill which enables you to tell your story to someone else, getting their reaction and advice, and helping you to think it out more clearly. If you don't understand something, ask questions. *But beware of talking too much and paying no heed to your listener.*

Listening is a much neglected skill which enables you to learn from the experience of others. Listen carefully, evaluating what you hear and checking it against reality. *Beware of people who spread poison, tell lies, or generally talk rubbish.*

Worrying can be a sensible skilled process, in which you think ahead and assess risks. If you don't have enough information, ask someone who does. *Beware of going round in a circle, worrying fruitlessly. If you can't find an answer, put it on hold until more information emerges, or until the time is ripe.*

Ignoring involves quite a skilled balance of probabilities. You take note of the risks but decide that it is more important to take action than to be totally safe. Alternatively you decide to relax and do nothing, rather than reacting to something. *But beware of ignoring significant risks that you have failed to consider properly.*

Exploring involves seeking out changes or new ideas. The skill lies in devising ways of trying things out, so that you can evaluate what happens. You have to do this not only with new experiences, but also with things that you are avoiding because of anxiety. *But beware of the stress of too many new things at a time.*

Keeping some parts of your life constant is good for your wellbeing, especially when you are trying to change other things. Your body in particular needs fairly regular habits, such as eating and sleeping times. The skill lies in distinguishing between a healthy habit and an unhealthy addictive one. *Beware of trying to enforce stability on other people, who really cannot stay the same just for your benefit.*

Caring for or helping someone is good for your own state of mind or well-being. Forgiving a person who has offended against you is likewise a healthy thing to do. The skill in caring is how to actually achieve some good, rather than just putting on a performance. *Beware the parasitic nature of some people who would abuse your good nature. And never forget a person's track record even if you have forgiven them for it.*

Accusing someone means that you identify them as the source of your problem. If their behaviour is unnecessary and unreasonable and they won't alter it, you are entitled to detach yourself from them or their influence. The same principle applies to other things which behave addictively or problematically, such as drugs, alcohol, food, money and sex. People or things that cause problems often add to this by making you feel guilty or at fault. The skill here is to put the blame back where it belongs. Toxic people are toxic, addictive substances are addictive, and you did not make them so. *However, beware of continually denigrating people and making false accusations.*

Striving to achieve your aims means working hard, rather than just waiting for things to drop into your lap. The skill here is making sure that you do achieve something, rather than just working for no result. Healthy exercise requires effort, discipline and persistence, and should produce benefits for your physical and mental well-being. *But beware of being over-conscientious, perfectionistic or excessively competitive.*

Taking gifts or help from others can be quite difficult for conscientious people, as they really hate owing anything. However, social groupings, as well as personal relationships, depend on this kind of give and take, so accept with gratitude, especially if you are in need. The skill is to postpone your repayment without guilt, or even to do something for someone else entirely. *But don't be a habitual or total parasite on anyone, even if you are dependent.*

Confessing is usually the best way to deal with your errors and faults. At the very least, you need to confess mistakes to yourself, so that you recognise the truth and will learn the necessary lessons. If someone else is affected, an apology or at least a confession will reduce any harm to your relationship. There is much skill in making an apology that will not be criticised for being insufficient or insincere. *But don't go too far the other way and make false confessions or extravagant and unbelievable apologies.*

Lying or covering things up is not always the evil option. For example white lies and diplomatic excuses are ways of not offending people, in situations where the truth is unnecessarily offensive. The skill is in knowing whether the truth will emerge, and whether anyone is interested in it. Next, there is nothing wrong with the human need for privacy. Here you are covering up aspects of yourself that do not need to be told. There is no extra truth in them. Finally, there is nothing wrong with the fact that no one can see or know your thoughts or feelings. That is simply the human condition. It would be wrong to over-expose yourself. *But don't cover up things that cannot be covered up. You will be found out.*

We all develop these skills quite naturally, through our

experience of life. Indeed it is a life-long process which never reaches perfection. Whether it can really be improved by deliberate teaching is something that requires extensive investigation. I do wish that I could have been better prepared during my childhood and adolescence, but fortunately it is never too late to learn.

BIBLIOGRAPHY

Bandura, Albert (1977). Social Learning Theory. Englewood Cliffs, NJ: Prentice-Hall.

Berman, Marc G. et al (2008). The cognitive benefits of interacting with nature. Psychological Science, 19, 12, 1207-1212.

Bishop, Sue (2006). Develop your assertiveness. London: Kogan Page.

Brown, M.L. et al (2011). Treatment of primary nocturnal enuresis in children: a review. Child: Care, Health and Development, 37, 2, 153-160.

Butler, Gillian (2008). Overcoming social anxiety and shyness. London: Constable and Robinson.

Cole, David A, et al (1998). A longitudinal look at the relation between depression and anxiety in children and adolescents. Journal of Consulting and Clinical Psychology, 66, 3, 451-460.

Fink, Max (2009). Electro-convulsive therapy: A guide for professionals and their patients. New York: Oxford University Press.

Forehand, R. et al (1998). Cumulative risk across family stressors: short- and long-term effects for adolescents. Journal of abnormal child psychology, 26, 2, 119-128.

Gateshead Grammar School website: www.gateshead-grammar.com

Goffman, E. (1961). Asylums: Essays on the social situation of mental patients and other inmates. New York: Doubleday Anchor.

Hamilton, S. (2010). Report for the Nursing and Midwifery Council on nursing skills for working with people with a mental health diagnosis. London: Rethink.

Hays, Peter (1964). New horizons in psychiatry. London: Penguin.

Howard, N.E. (1959). Standard handbook for telescope making. New York: Crowell.

Kohn, Alfie (1993). No Contest: The case against competition. New York: Houghton Mifflin.

Lee, K. and Ashton, M.C. (2005). Psychopathy, Machiavellianism, and Narcissism in the five-factor model and the HEXACO model of personality structure. Personality and Individual Differences, 38, 1571-1582.

McCrae, Robert R. and Costa, Paul T. (2003). Personality in adulthood: A five-factor theory perspective. New York: The Guilford Press.

Nettle, Daniel (2003). Intelligence and class mobility in the British population. British Journal of Psychology, 94, 551-561.

Oishi, Shigehiro and Schimmack, Ulrich (2010). Residential mobility, well-being and mortality. Journal of Personality and Social Psychology. 98, 6, 980-994.

Pinker, Steven (2002). The Blank Slate: The modern denial of human nature. London: Penguin.

Platt, Stephen and Salter, Denis (1987). A comparative investigation of health workers' attitudes towards parasuicide. Social Psychiatry, 22, 202-208.

Shelton, Katherine H. and Harold, Gordon T. (2008). Pathways between interparental conflict and adolescent psychological adjustment. Journal of Early Adolescence, 28, 555-582.

Smith, G. Alan (2011). From tests to therapy: a personal history of clinical psychology. Leicester: Matador.

Snaith, R.P. and Taylor, C. M. (1985). Irritability: definition, assessment and associated factors. British Journal of Psychiatry, 147, 127-136.

Watt, Dominic (2002). I don't speak with a Geordie accent, I speak, like, the Northern accent: Contact induced levelling in the Tyneside vowel system. Journal of Sociolinguistics, 6, 1, 44-63.

Weir, Kirsten (2011). Our forgotten years. New Scientist, 30 April, 42-45.

Wooldridge, Adrian (1995). Measuring the mind: Education and psychology in England c.1860 – c.1990. Cambridge University Press.